"This Was Logging!"

This Was Logging!

Selected Photographs of Darius Kinsey

Text by
Ralph W. Andrews

77 Lower Valley Road, Atglen, PA 19310

Published by Schiffer Publishing, Ltd.
77 Lower Valley Road
Atglen, PA 19310
Please write for a free catalog.
This book may be purchased from the publisher.
Please include $2.95 postage.
Try your bookstore first.

We are interested in hearing from authors
with book ideas on related subjects.

Originally published 1954 by Superior Publishing Company
Copyright 1982 © by Ralph W. Andrews.
Copyright 1984 © by Ralph W. Andrews.

Printed in the United States of America.
ISBN: 0-88740-035-3

DEDICATED

to the Pioneering Spirit of
the early lumbermen of
the Pacific Northwest
and to
Darius Kinsey
who preserved it
in picture

❧

FOREWORD

NO INDUSTRY in the Pacific Northwest has been closer to the hearts of the people than lumbering. It concerns trees which are growing things and for which people have a deep affection. It concerns great enterprise and activity in producing a basic commodity in which a large share of the people have had a part. It concerns the harvesting of a crop which has been vital to the growth of the nation and other nations and has returned untold dollar wealth to the Pacific Northwest.

Now the Big Woods have gone and since the people have not been able to preserve the trees themselves, they turn to their memories and those shoddy substitutes... other people's memories. They want to glory in the great days of logging and try to find pictures of them. Even those who have no direct relationship to Pacific Northwest lumbering are interested, for pictures of this nature are evidence of transition and historically invaluable.

So it seems strange that no one has set about to produce a book of such pictures. Many efforts of Northwest history and Americana have contained various photographs of timbering but no one has attempted to round up enough good photographs to create a book acceptable to a publisher and the public. However, it would be a colossal task and it is very doubtful if the result would ever be more than a hodge podge of subjects and good and bad photography.

This volume becomes possible first, because the logging industry had one excellent "official" photographer who had the good sense to preserve most of his negatives in a sealed vault and second, because a photographer of today had the wisdom to realize the public deserves to share in this store of treasure.

"This Was Logging!" then is the writer's selection of the best of Darius Kinsey. When Jesse E. Ebert approached him with the fact that he had purchased the 8000-odd 11" x 14" negatives and prints, and wanted to do something more with them, plans were made to build a book. Albert Salisbury and his Superior Publishing Company in Seattle entered the plan and took over the publication responsibility. In this way a story which might well have been lost is told here and promises to live for generations.

This book is not a "complete" anything. It is not a history of logging photographically or otherwise. It contains about 200 reproductions of outstanding photographs Darius Kinsey took in the woods, a brief biography of the man and a few highlights of text to give meaning and interest to the pictures. At least five times as many good photographs had to be omitted.

It should be mentioned that first and last, Darius Kinsey was a photographer, as Stewart Holbrook has said . . . "in the Matthew Brady tradition." He was not a recorder of data about his pictures. It was enough for him to get a beautiful, realistic image without filling notebooks with names and data about the setting. As a result the information contained in the captions under the reproductions has been gleaned from various sources and in many cases is general rather than specific.

In securing material for the text, it was necessary to presume upon the time of busy people and let me hasten to acknowledge the willing help of those mentioned here, all of whom I am sure felt a certain responsibility to the public. The primary source of information about Darius Kinsey was the lady who shared his adult life, Mrs. Darius Kinsey, who graciously searched her memory.

Much technical data was supplied by Kenneth A. Schell of Skagit Steel and Iron Works; Gerald and Francis Frink of Washington Iron Works; Beaumont Newhall, curator of George Eastman House in Rochester, New York. References to published material are given where used.

For stimulating ideas and encouragement, let me publicly thank Northwest writers James Stevens and Stewart Holbrook; Peyton Phillips, Robert E. Mahaffey, Donald Bowman, Palmer G. Lewis, David Pollock, and other individuals and publications which have cooperated editorially.

RALPH W. ANDREWS

"This Was Logging!"

MAN AND HIS INDUSTRY. Darius Kinsey was well established as "picture maker of the woods" when this view was made in 1914. Kinsey holds Press Graflex camera, standing under the 11 x 14 Eastman View camera with which he did most of his work at this time. The especially made tripod was extendable to 12 feet. Beside Kinsey is Folmer and Schwing Cirkut camera which swung by clockwork during exposure for panoramic view. Double lens camera is Stereoscopic Premo and big one above it 20 x 24 Empire State view camera, both made by Rochester Optical Co. until 1913. Note double tripod to support great weight. Plate holder in foreground with two glass negatives weighed over twenty-five pounds. This photograph has been accepted by Beaumont Newhall, curator of George Eastman House in Rochester.

1895 portrait of DARIUS KINSEY
by Kinsey & Kinsey—Woolley, Nooksack,
Arlington, Snoqualmie, Washington
Official Artists, L. S. and E. R. R.

Darius Kinsey sketches George Washington.
He brought his crayons and easel to Washington but soon discarded them for the more
satisfying camera.

SURVIVOR OF A THOUSAND DEATHS. Character study of Indian doctor of Snohomish tribe, nicknamed "Fall City Doc," who lived 130 years although supposed to die when any patient did. Darius Kinsey made this candid shot as the old doctor was carving paddles in his shack, well preserved in dirt of the earthy and other kinds. Beside officiating at burials and attempting crude cures with herbs, potions and steam baths, he taught young Indians to carve and fashion canoes. Line [at top left] is crack in 11 x 14 glass plate.

WEATHER PROPHETESS. Pilchuck Julia was 100 years old, toothless and almost blind, when Darius Kinsey photographed her, wrinkles and rags, in 1920. This Snohomish Indian woman was a familiar figure in the woods and hop fields and known all over the Puget Sound country for her uncannily accurate weather predictions. A favorite saying was—"Pilchuck Julia says we'll have snow three squaws deep." [Right] Sammamish Indian who preferred being photographed in this blanket rather than his natural gear.

DEE KINSEY was fond of saying "You aren't a logger until you own a dollar watch and have your picture taken with a tree." Kinsey saw untold numbers of big trees, logger characters and some watches. There was the story of the mild mannered, simple hearted bucker who carried his Ingersoll, neatly protected, in an empty Copenhagen box in the edge of which a hole had been punched for the stem. Loggers used to ask him, "Well, Lars—what time you got by the snoose box?" Lars would dredge up the box from the depths of his pants pocket, carefully take off the tin cover and solemnly declaim the hour, always adding the ominous words, "And so much nearer eternity."

TRAPPINGS OF AN ERA. The Kinsey home and studio in Sedro-Woolley with 4th of July trimmings—about 1900. Mrs. Tabitha Kinsey is shown on right at round-spindle fence. She was a faithful dark-room assistant to Dee Kinsey for the better part of 50 years. Rattan chair on left porch is shown in interior. Note high bicycles on studio porch. [Right] Time-exposed self portrait of Tib and Dee Kinsey in their studio home. It was furnished in the prevailing fashion from bear rug to satin bows and fish net hangings. Clock shelf was preempted by Kinsey's early prints and family portraits. Sheet music on Cornish organ is song and cake walk, "The Coon's Breach of Promise." At its base is Kinsey's painting of Washington seacoast. Newspaper on his lap is Seattle Post-Intelligencer.

When Kinsey came to the Pacific Northwest in 1885, as a 20-year-old boy, he found romance behind every big tree. The country was raw, the land covered with dense forests from which logs were being dragged in endless procession. Farms were being opened up in the stump land, saw-mills built on the rivers, railroads coming in and trading ships sailing out of Aberdeen, Tacoma, Seattle, Everett and Bellingham.

The logging camps were cutting the finest timber ever to come out of the Northwest— prime fir, cedar and spruce logs, six, eight, twelve feet in diameter. There were probably 250 timber companies operating around Puget Sound Columbia River and Washington seacoast. Within a year, Darius Kinsey made his decision — to photograph all this energy and enterprise.

Darius Kinsey was not a genius. He was a

skilled technician who thoroughly understood
his subject. He was an intent, diligent worker of
single purpose, full of courage with a fine sense
of adventure. There was a little of the artist in
him and a little showmanship but the never-
ceasing drive to capture on plate the fallers,
buckers, bull skinners, choker setters and high
riggers created the successful Kinsey. He was a
master at making a small sifting of dim light do

the work of bright sunshine. He had no light
meter and little regard for the new flash powder.
The patience with which he worked, using crude
equipment, experimental lenses, plates and developers, was the wonder of his work.

Kinsey was not the best known photographer
in the Pacific Northwest because he was not a
commercial photographer in the strict sense.
Asahel Curtis, Webster and Stevens, Cress-Dale

Hop picking furnished young Darius Kinsey a livelihood until the timber took hold of him. Only white man in this group of Siwash Indians near Mt. Si [North Bend] is shown in center with umbrella. Hops grow on twelve foot high frames. In fall vines are cut down and blossoms harvested.

[Left] Siwash types with baskets of harvested hop blossoms. This glass negative was badly damaged.

and others came to mind first. But that was because Kinsey stayed with the timber and became unquestionably the best recorder of logs and lumber in action. He has been criticized as not getting the kind of picture machinery and lumber firms wanted. This can be excused on one basis. Darius Kinsey never felt he was working for anybody but the people in the picture—the loggers themselves. As a consequence it was difficult to hire him on assignment. If he was taking photographs of men in some camp he would include shots of donkeys or skidding apparatus or cook houses. But always he was on his own assignment to picture life and logging methods in the grand scale.

Darius Kinsey was born in Marysville, Missouri, in 1871 and a sense of adventure was born with him. While a small boy his mother would call "D-rius" and he naturally came by the nickname "Dee." He started earning money in the coal mines which was a blind, frustrating occupation. There was a creative urge in this Missouri boy, at the time expressed in certain facility with crayons. He sketched buildings and cows, and, with less success, people, particularly the heads of famous men of history. This turned him toward photography as a more faithful type of reproduction. The fad was just coming into public play and it appealed to Darius. However the desire to follow the camera as a lifework did not manifest itself until Darius had broken with the Middle West and followed the trail of Ezra Meeker.

An older brother, Alfred, had settled in Snoqualmie, Washington, and wrote glowing letters of opportunities in the new land. Darius was easily persuaded and at length landed wide-eyed in the frontier town which was already the seat of one of the largest lumbering operations in the state. Darius was twenty years old, small of stature and as full of energy as a colt. For a year

Totem pole carved by William Shelton, Tulalip Indian, to detail tribal history.

he and Alfred worked in the hop fields, side by side with Indian men and women, pulling the vines and stripping off the blossoms which were a prime crop. Even at a dollar a day the pair saved enough money to buy lots in Snoqualmie and build a small hotel—Mt. Si Hotel—named after the big rock which juts out of the Cascade Mountains in that area.

Then the virus which attacks even the wary, struck Darius Kinsey. Snoqualmie had a photographic studio through which he learned of a Mrs. Spalding in Seattle who would teach him the fundamentals of camera operation. He went to Seattle, took lessons, bought a 6½" x 8½" camera and he was in business.

Kinsey, of course, was impressed by the big city of Seattle and smaller but thriving Tacoma, thirty country miles to the south. There were little towns up and down Puget Sound, dotted here and there in gaps between the timbered hills and nestled in sheltered coves. But Seattle was the hub of industry, the focal point of ships from world ports and thousands of fortune seekers from the east—the bustling, alert, green, raw city grown from a few clusters of shacks in 1875 to more than 60,000 citizens in 1885.

Here were docks teeming with trade—ocean vessels bringing in clothing, food and people, loading out lumber and flour for Australia, Japan and China—big freighters with Chinese crews tied up along waterfronts that smelled of coal smoke, tar and tide flats. Everywhere were the rattle of wagons on paving stones, the clatter of boots on wooden sidewalks, the shouts of teamsters and stevedores.

(Continued on page 21)

The Kinseys just before they moved to Seattle. [Below] Kinsey's journeys into the timber and away from developing and printing facilities made necessary a detailed record of film shipments home. Finished prints usually had to be shipped to him in the woods and delivered to men in camps. This page indicated films and prints for Bloedel-Donovan, Dempsey, Lyman, Wood and Knight.

Early Logging
in British Columbia

AT COMOX on Vancouver Island, the Minnesota logger J. D. McCormick built the Comox Railway and rafted logs to Vancouver mills. Robert Filberg was manager of this operation. The Pendleton brothers were also logging on the Island, the son of one brother, Ross Pendleton, becoming manager of Alberni-Pacific logging operations. The Victoria Lumber and Mfg. Co., owned by the Palmer interests, had a mill at Ladysmith and built a logging road into the Cowichan Lake country. John Humbird was manager later. Charley Cobb had timber in the Campbell Lake area and founded the International Timber Co., with Charles Killsche as manager. The name was later changed to Elk River Logging Co. Richard Cobb, the son, was manager.

J. H. Bloedel had large operations on the Island—Bloedel, Stewart and Welsh, near Menzies Bay, one at Port Alberni up the Franklin River, and another at Great Central Lake. In 1908, at Alert Bay, Stracey and Garland built a logging road into Numpkish Lake, rafting logs into Beaver Cove and towing them south.

There were a number of railroad operations on the mainland, up the Fraser River—Heaps Bros. at Dryden, Abernathy and Lougheed at Pacific Mills—and on the Straits, Powell River Co., Brooks-Scanlon-O'Brian at Stillwater, Rat Portage Logging Co., and Capilano Timber Co. at Grassy Bay.

TOTEM POLE
Opposite side of William Shelton's totem pole

One of Kinsey's best known pictures. Enlargements hang on the office walls of many Pacific Northwest lumber firms and hundreds of smaller prints have been sold over the country. It depicts a team of 12 bulls on the 1892 skid road of Bryan and Reid, pioneer loggers near Arlington, Washington. Fallen spruce has been sawed through for access of yoked and chained bulls. Logs were freed of bark to make them slide easier over the pole-studded skid road. Alex and Robert Polson, of Grays Harbor, in one of the world's finest stands of fir, were among the first to use

bull teams. But they were quick to see the economical advantage of steam. Their booming grounds were on the middle fork of the Hoquiam River and logs were towed to Hoquiam and Aberdeen mills.

Flanking the downtown activity, were Seattle's famous "seven hills," timber already fallen in front of the ever-expanding arc of brick and frame houses, stores and warehouses. Every day brought more people — by wagons, stages, ship and train, as the Northern Pacific came to the end of its transcontinental run.

Tacoma was the western terminus of this rail line and Seattle fought hard to win this privilege. But the N. P. men were fighters too and started the movement to change the name of Mt. Rainier to Mt. Tacoma — from the Indian word "Tahoma" meaning "snow peak." The controversy made bitter enemies of the Seattle and Tacoma citizenry and died a lingering death only after the N. P. decided definitely to make Seattle its terminus.

And it was into Seattle's "skidroad" that loggers came after long months in the bush, loaded with the stuff that brought fancy women, gamblers and whiskey salesmen. Saloons, honky tonks and girl shows flashed their gaudy banners. Red lights burned over dingy doorways and darning needles tapped on dirty window panes— "Come on boys — trip around the world for a dollar!"

The boy Darius Kinsey saw the skidroad as a spectator. He saw it as the logger's safety valve. What if this hard working woodsman did blow his stake of two or three hundred dollars in a few nights and get a boot kick in the pants for thanks? Didn't he see all his friends, get a chance to win money, girls and drinks on the house? Wasn't he seeing the bright lights instead of the smoky lanterns of the bunkhouse? This was high living. If it didn't last long, it was educational.

Kinsey saw all this gaudy glitter and many business opportunities in the city. But he was a craftsman and he was learning to photograph people and things. It was all right to come to Seattle once in a while to catch up on latest developments and to buy supplies but up there on the mountain streams and canyon sides was beautiful timber and thousands of men ready to be photographed at their falling, bucking and loading—at fifty cents a head.

(Continued on page 25)

BULLS OF THE WOODS. Oxen on landing at A. S. Kerry's camp east of Renton in 1893. In 1897 Kerry founded Kerry Mill Co. at Kerriston and in 1913 built a logging road from Columbia River into Nehalem Valley, boring tunnel into mountains. With C. D. Stimson, he built a sawmill in Ballard and a railroad — the Marysville and Northern — to Bryant where Chris Gilson was logging superintendent.

Quoting from Dave James' description in Simpson Logging Co.'s "Big Skookum": "The bulls were brought from great distances, chained and yoked together, goaded into effort by bellowing men who could be heard for miles. Boys going into the woods for the first time were given the job of swabbing whale oil or crude oil on the skids to help the logs slip. This was about the only help anyone gave the bulls. The puncher, that master of profanity, consigned them to Burning Eternity a hundred times daily. Of all the types of power brought into the timber, only the bull teams served man's stomach. The accident victims could be eaten. Loudest cuss ever heard in a bunkhouse was when a logger bit into a yoke buckle in his beef roast."

[Following page] Bulls were kept in corrals and barns at night, shod, with two plates to each cloven hoof, on Sundays and days when weather or snow was too bad to work. This photograph is early morning scene at camp getting teams on skid road. Bull puncher is shown with goad in hand. Fallers are mixed in with skidding crew.

The "B" brand on the oxen's flanks was not for "beef" or "bulls" in this case but stood for Berggen's Logging Camp, Lake McMurray, Washington. There is no specific record of loggers having to protect their skidding machinery by branding it. So Darius Kinsey, making this photograph in 1896, decided to do his own branding on the negative. Fir log is 14 feet in diameter.

At first, because he was feeling his way into photography and because it required little traveling expense, Darius was satisfied to take pictures of family groups and wedding parties. People were interested and if they had the money, Dee Kinsey was interested. At this stage he made one of his longest trips to photograph the Pritts family at Nooksack, a young and comely member being Tabitha Mae. Friendship and romance developed and on October 8, 1896, Dee Kinsey and Tib Pritts were married. He was 25 at the time. Let's see what the *Nooksack Reporter* said about the event.

"Married—Thursday, October 8th, at the residence of the bride's parents at Nooksack, by the Rev. J. L. Parmeter, Miss Tabitha M. Pritts of Nooksack and Mr. D. R. Kinsey of Snoqualmie. The bride, who is one of the most popular belles of the Nooksack Valley, looked very pretty in old-gold cashmere tastefully trimmed with silk and ribbons. The groom, well known as the Lake Shore photographer, was handsomely attired in regulation black.

"The wedding day was the 42d anniversary of the marriage of the bride's parents, Mr. and Mrs. S. A. Pritts. A wedding breakfast followed the ceremony; and the friends accompanied the happy couple to the Lake Shore depot, where they started for a tour of the Sound cities, under the usual send-off of rice, old slippers, etc. They received numerous handsome and useful presents. Besides the parents of the bride there were present—John Pritts and family, Mr. and Mrs. Jess Tucker, A. M. and D. L. Germain and families, Mr. and Mrs. John Berg, Mrs. Lee, Mrs. S. Berg and sons David, Jacob and Aaron, Mr. and

"A bunch of the boys" in an 1892 logging camp bunkhouse. Crowded into small quarters while their wet clothes were drying on lines over the stoves, loggers had little to do after ten or twelve hours in the woods but play cards in the lamp-lit gloom and sleep exhaustedly. No movies, no radio, no library—no wonder the food had to be good and abundant. If it went down grade, so did the men, packs on their backs. Bunkhouses were warmed by the proverbial pot-bellied, stove. Loggers washed socks and woolen underwear in kerosene cans filled with water and heated on stoves. Some Sundays might be spent hunting deer and graybacks, both of which were plentiful.

POWER IN REPOSE. This photograph typifies the relentless strength inherent in early logging operations. Bull puncher and oxen relax momentarily, sullenly conscious of their ability to get any job done, no matter how tough. Note grease on logs to help skid of shingle bolts slide more easily.

Mrs. Butterfield, Mrs. P. Gillies, Jr., and Miss Selma Swanson, Mrs. Sleasman and Mr. L. Bushby."

The Kinseys decided then to set up shop in Sedro-Woolley, which community had just been legalized by the consolidation of the two towns, Sedro and Woolley. They built a home with a sky-lighted studio. The general plan was for Darius to go into the logging camps, take photographs of the men working at their various jobs —and any others the company wanted, such as a big log or some spectacular operation—and in some manner get the photographic plates back to Mrs. Kinsey for processing.

Altogether this was a major undertaking, but worth the gamble. He acquired a horse and wagon resembling an early-type milk rig in which the driver stood up to handle the reins. He stocked this iron-tired chariot with the big camera, home-made tripods extendable to twelve

feet, three or four weeks' supply of glass plates and the newer "color blind" film, folder of sample prints to show men what they might expect, hammer and nails for building scaffolds to hold cameras, shipping boxes, etc. He had to determine which camps were running, number of men working, what road, if any, there was into the camp and whether or not the foreman would let him take pictures.

The enterprise got underway, jerkily and uncertain at the start. From the Kinsey Studio, Kinsey made his forays into the timber. Early in the morning he would load up the wagon—later is was a Ford and still later a Franklin—and perhaps by noon would make his destination. After making arrangements with the woods boss, he unpacked and got on location up some mountain slope by walking or gas speeder with the laborious job of getting the big camera set up and maneuvering the willing but unwieldy subjects.

27

HAY BURNERS ON ROAD. [Left, above] Twelve horses hauling logs through old burn. Horses quickly replaced oxen for yarding after turn of the century as being faster, more easily handled and not armed with horns. Logs in this photo were loaded on skids instead of being chained end-to-end and dragged down skid road. [Left, below] Here are two four-horse teams with light wheel wagons at log dump. [Above] Six-horse team on early skid road. At tail end of logs is raft-like "pig" which carried tools and buckets and one or more of crew to keep logs from snagging.

After the "timber stiffs" had been shot, the return trip to camp had to be made and then came the really complicated task of getting the exposed plates back to Mrs. Kinsey, fifty or a hundred miles away, for processing. Usually he packed the plates into the original wooden boxes and if he had further work in camp, paid a logger to pack the load down to some expressing point. Or he did this himself before starting out for the next camp, always faced with the necessity of returning to this spot, distributing prints and collecting fifty cents from each logger. The woods-to-studio liaison was further handicapped by snow and fire season shutdowns. With some

lumbering outfits, Kinsey could get checks covering all photographs made, the company deducting individual amounts from the men's pay.

Back in the studio Tib Kinsey had her own difficulties. Mixed developers were almost unknown. There was a great variation in the density of negatives due to errors in time calculations and many of them show the liberal use of intensifier solutions. Mrs. Kinsey well recalls her husband's insistence that each print be washed sixteen times to prevent discoloration. "We had our children and other help in the studio," she says. "When Dee thought the wash-

(Continued on page 36)

END OF THE HAUL for ten-horse team in 1907. Logs were skidded to river bank landing where rolling jacks were used to get them into the water. "Grease monkey" at head of team carries swab and pail of heavy oil for greasing cross logs. Curved line at left is crack in glass negative. [Below] Old single-drum donkey loading logs on wagon. Line horse ready to start back for another hitch of logs.

Hand Logging

THE anything-but-gentle art of logging big trees by hand was not only the first method of logging but will probably be the last. All a person needs is a couple of screw or pump jacks, a fairly steep show where logs will slide directly into water, and the agility and guts of a kangaroo.

There was a limited amount of hand logging done on Hood Canal and the Olympic Peninsula, more in the British Columbia islands where it is practiced in a limited way today. Some loggers operating today with steam and gas equipment, began the business in hand logging. Present day hand loggers make passable wages, but there was a day, around the '20s, when partners could make $25 to $35 a day each. There is no possible way to propel logs by hand, but by falling them so they will pitch headlong over a cliff or down a slope into the water, a pair of solid men can make a living. They can even hand log when the tree falls and grounds itself, by means of the hand jacks.

Generally the method is like this. A cross-ribbing of short logs is laid on the slope under the trees to be felled, to act as skids. The tree is felled and it lies on the skids, with only the lower branches keeping it from sliding down. Beginning at the butt, the top branches are lopped off one by one close to the bark.

Then the jack is set and the tree rolled over to get the lower branches on top. At any point in the operation now, the log may suddenly take off and even with a kangaroo jump, a man may be caught by a branch or knot or by the log pivoting on a high spot and side swiping the logger. In case the tree does not start down, another jack is set under the small end of the tree down the slope and very slowly and carefully raised. And when the tree lugs free, it springs into action like a mountain cat. Whoever has been operating the jack had better be in the air before the tree is.

On a half mile or mile slope, the tree will "run" at an inconceivable speed and with tremendous crushing power. Trees rushing headlong down steep pitches have been known to ram through larger trees or split them from roots to top. Smaller trees struck by this catapulting log may fly into the air like bowling pins.

The story is told of a hand logger who invented a hydraulic jack that operated on alcohol. With a partner he contracted to log a certain hillside stand of timber. After a few days the jack wouldn't work. Examination showed it full of water. That was when he had discovered how his partner had kept himself drunk for three days.

Horse team stops on 1894 skid road of Ferguson and McKilligan near Arlington to be photographed with crew falling 12-foot fir. Picture is a study in brute strength and mustaches. The "dogger" on the skidding crew was called such as he carried a steel pinch bar and wooden maul to pry dogs out of logs, shown at end of chain in foreground. [Opposite page] Horses have hauled logs, notched for bridge timbers, to railroad landing.

1905 view of ten horses hauling ten-foot spruce log on skid road.

Dee Kinsey left no record of the location of this roofed stump, nor information as to what, if more than a tourist curiosity, it was used for. It was a big cedar once

One Camp Was Like This in 1921

ONE of the big lumbering companies described its woods operation in this manner, thirty-three years ago:

"We maintain three logging camps, averaging from 125 to 160 men each. In each camp are thirteen cars, in addition to outbuildings, all steam heated, electrically lighted, with complete plumbing, hot and cold water. Two dining cars, capable of seating one hundred men each, occupy the angle of a switch, where they are joined together by a common platform. One train, which forms a complete community, begins with a combination car, with a boiler supplying steam and heat to run a 7-kilowatt turbine with current for electric light and ice machine. The car has a sleeping room for the operator, a large dry room for clothes, a room with four zinc-lined shower baths and hot and cold water day and night. In the cook car is a half-ton ice machine, and the latest construction in cooling apparatus, a box ten feet long, eight feet high and five feet wide, containing brine tubes, with power from a 1½ horsepower electric motor. There are three rooms: (1) meat house, with cooling equipment, meat block and storage of meat for two hundred men; (2) supply room for canned goods, sugar, flour; (3) kitchen, with ranges, sinks, serving tables, cupboards. In addition to the two dining cars, there is an office car, with sleeping room for the timekeeper and foreman, also a large commissary room, and a supply room for pipes, fittings and axes. There is a library car, with card room, reading room with writing desk, drafting room, two rooms for scalers with two beds in each, and accommodation for chief engineer and cruiser. There is a compartment car with seven rooms well ventilated, with wash bowl, hot and cold water, and an abundance of light through large windows.

"The sleeping cars, of which there are six in each camp, are a distinct triumph in the development of modern logging. Time was when each logger carried his roll of blankets as he traveled from place to place. His quarters were unsanitary, and the logger was no better than his surrounding, often filthy and infested with vermin. In each of the six sleeping cars, are four compartments, each with accommodations for eight men. There are double bunks, felt mattress, two sheets with cotton blanket under bottom sheet, pillow and pillow case, two wool blankets zero gray, and over the top a bed cover of brown canvas. On the top bunk between the mattress and the spring is an extra bed cover. This sleeping equipment comes close to representing the last word in supplying the needs of camp life.

"The cars are fourteen feet wide by sixty-four feet long, with heavy sills and heavy double flooring. They measure eight feet to the top of the sill where the roof goes up, and then there is a rise of two feet for ventilation. They are painted pearl gray inside, and box car red with white trimmings on the outside. Each of the cars is on wheels, ready to be moved whenever the progress of cutting the timber requires a shifting of camp. Such a shifting took place during the first week in July, when Camp 4 was moved from its old location to a point much higher up in the timber. The cars were taken up the incline and along one of the laterals— and the job was completed in a day and a half.

"Accessory buildings for each of the camps include a house for the superintendent, a house for extra bedding, filing house, a house for waitresses, blacksmith shop, oil house and sand house. These houses are built on skids. A most important part is a comfort station, with modern plumbing and running water, paralleling the like accommodations at any first-class hotel."

30,000 feet of lumber forms one wall of this logger's shack.

NATURE AND MEN. Here is graphic reason why Dee Kinsey needed a special tripod for elevation. Photo above is copy of 1908 stereoptican print. Kinsey is shown on jerry-built scaffold ten or twelve feet from ground to raise 100-pound 20 x 24 camera to level of undercut in big cedar. View opposite is one taken at this time showing same tree with men in altered positions. Later he developed the very high tripod for undistorted perspective. This cedar is supposed to have been the largest tree in the State of Washington, measuring 76 feet in circumference, 1 ½ feet from ground and was photographed many times.

ing process was being slighted, he put sixteen pebbles out in a row and told the girls to move one out of line with each washing. Afterwards he built a more permanent numbering system over the wash trays."

From the starting of this pioneering effort, it can be seen just what sort of man the woodsmen were dealing with. He was a determined, studious young man with well planted ideas. When he had

resolved himself to a situation or aim, he drove straight toward it with fervor and flame. This forthright quality was further strengthened by a solid moral sense which turned him naturally toward religion. He was Sunday School superintendent in the Methodist church for many years. Was it coincidence then that set up the Kinsey Studio in Sedro-Woolley next door to a church? It was certainly this adherence to stout

FOREST GIANT. Fine contrast between mill-run timber and outstanding growth in mature forest. Douglas fir being cut by five men was 14 feet in diameter. Smaller trees would be good merchantable timber these days. Timber was so thick in rain forests, it was necessary to take all of it out. If any was left it would eventually die.

MOTHER GOOSE HOUSE. This logger just couldn't get away from trees. In 1901 he packed his living into this red cedar stump. One of the world's most durable woods, Western red cedar withstands rot and shrinkage for hundreds of years. Big cedars are also overripe and hollow at the core. Other such stumps have been used for storehouses for tools, for tourist curiosities, and one utilized as a logging camp post office. Even today a stump near Sedro-Woolley, Washington, is occupied by a man as a dwelling. Holes in tree were made for fallers' spring boards.

principles that caused him to refuse any picture takings on Sunday. That was a rule he never violated, in the woods and out. Toting the heavy cameras in and out of log camps was hard work. So when Sunday came, he used that seventh day for what it was intended.

The hard working young fellow who was to become an ace timber photographer had many relieving qualities. He was generous to a fault, very kind and considerate to his wife and later his children. He had a droll, dry sense of humor but knew its limits and the danger of levity when serious business was demanded. He was "death on liquor" and never made an exception in refusing it. Many times he was offered drinks but always laughed the drinker away. He was

Early Logging in California

THE Timberman, an international lumber journal, Portland, Oregon, of October, 1949, contained an informative account of pioneer lumbering along the southern Sierras from which the following is quoted.

"Many of the huge sequoias were more than 20 feet in diameter and over 250 feet tall. One 12-foot tree, 251 feet long when felled, produced about 100,000 feet of lumber. There is a report of one acre with a million board feet of standing timber. One big tree was converted into lumber in Tulare County in 1890 at a cost of $1,500. The lumber was sold for $2,500, yielding a net profit of $1,000 from the single tree.

"The wood of these giants is not strong, but like that of its relative, the coast redwood, is resistant to decay. It was used for siding, interior finish, shingles, posts, grape stakes and pencil stock. Some was exported, and a quantity was shipped to Eastern markets.

"Because of the large size of these trees and the brashiness of the wood, it was necessary to build a bed for them before they were felled. This job often took two days for a crew of about seven men. Usually, the bottom cut of the undercut was sawed by hand and the undercut chopped out. Sometimes powder was used to make part of the undercut, which was then finished with axes. The saws used were more than 25 feet, and it took two days to a week to get the large trees down. The thick bark was peeled before the trees were bucked into logs.

"The Madera Flume & Trading Co. built a narrow-gauge logging railroad and started using a 10-ton, geared locomotive in about 1892. The locomotive was freighted up the steep mountain roads to the mill by teams. Other companies in this area used railroads for logging in later years.

"The first drum donkeys used for logging California were on the Madera Sugar Pine Co. operation in 1900. At the same time, large bull donkeys were used in place of the teams on the log chutes. After the turn of the century, steam donkeys and horses were the chief means of logging until the advent of the tractor. There was some use of big wheels and two-wheel dollies with horses.

"The expense of transporting logs down the steep mountain east of Fresno had a large part in the problems of the Sugar Pine Lumber Co. Transportation in this region was difficult from the first. Initially, lumber, shakes, posts and shingles were hauled with mules and ox teams out of the mountains, through uncut timber and brush. Large trees were tied behind the wagons as safety drags on the steep trails. To overcome this transportation problem, three lumber flumes were built, each more than 50 miles long.

"The first of these was started by the California Lumber Co., which built a two-saw, circular steam mill in 1872 on the headwaters of the Fresno River. This company failed in 1874 and was taken over by the Madera Flume & Trading Co. which eventually operated the mills with a combined production of three million feet per month. The flume was completed in the middle '70s and, after later additions, extended 65 miles from the mill in the mountains down to the railroad in the valley. The terminus at the railroad had had no previous development. The construction of the flume resulted in the birth of the present community of 9,000, called Madera (meaning 'timber' or 'wood' in Spanish).

"The second flume was completed at the end of the century by the Kings River Lumber Co. It ran from the mills on the Kings River down to Sanger near Fresno. It was eventually about 62 miles long.

"Both communities at the ends of the flumes claimed the title of 'the longest flume in the world,' and early writers gave various lengths for each of them. Each was V-shaped and took about two years to build. Good quality boards were needed to prevent leaks and many timbers were used for trestles, bridges and supports on the steep mountain sides. The Madera flume was 46 inches across and had 36-inch sides. It is reported to have required 5,700,000 feet of lumber and 2,100 kegs of nails. The width of the 1½-inch sides of the Kings River flume increased as it neared the railroad at Sanger. The water from the flumes was used for irrigation in the valley.

"The flumes cost about $300,000 each, and each had an approximate capacity of 250,000 board feet per day. The lumber was air seasoned or run through dry kilns before it went down the flume. At Hume there were two huge dry kilns, with a capacity of two million feet at one time. Each of the firms had a planing mill and box factory.

"Iron clamps held the boards in blocks about a foot thick and 20 to 28 feet long while they were flumed. These 'clamps of lumber' were tied together in units of six on leaving the Kings River operation. Further along the route, additional units were tied together by the 'flume herders.' These men maintained stations at junctions or other critical points to prevent jams. Their food supplies were floated down the flume to them.

"Inspections were made of the flume in a boat. Prior to the inspection trip a block of wood, called a 'joker,' was nailed on the flumed lumber. The herders were notified ahead of time, and they would phone when the joker passed their station. Thus, the inspector was reasonably sure the inspection could be made safely.

"The third largest flume in the area was built from Shaver Lake to Clovis, close to Fresno, by the Fresno Flume & Irrigation Company. The boards were flumed individually on this operation. The company cut about 450 million feet and flumed as much more from other, smaller mills in the area."

wrapped up in his work—lived, ate, slept in the woods with his photographs.

The forests in all these regions were generally ripe for cutting—Douglas fir, spruce and cedar averaging 500 years old, hemlock considered a waste wood, good only for skidroad logs and temporary camp construction. Forests came down to the edge of rivers, lakes and Puget Sound. There, logging operations began, the camps and mills eating their way back. If logs were not cut here, they were dumped into the water, rafted to Puget Sound mills and loaded on timber vessels.

At this time there were five main logging areas in Washington—the Skagit River area in which Darius Kinsey lived; the Snoqualmie River area farther south, east of Seattle to the Cascade Range; the Olympic Peninsula, from the coast to Hood Canal; the Grays Harbor and Willapa Harbor district; the Mt. Rainier area which included the Chehalis River.

Undercut of 10-foot fir completed, fallers take breather. Kinsey made use of every bit of light as there was little of it in the dense rain forests. Bark of this tree was easily a foot thick and allowed spring boards to be wedged in tightly. Even so, footing was none too solid when swinging heavy axes. Bottle on left is saw oil—on right, water for drinking. Fallers were not always giants. A common type was the gaunt, rangy Norwegian, Finn, or Pole.

FALLING FOREST GIANTS. [Left] There were more than 600 years of slow growth in this big fir, 51 feet in circumference four feet from the ground, with bark over a foot thick. Crosscut saws, even as long as 14 feet, were often not long enough to draw through the cut. They were sometimes cut in the middle and another saw brazed in between the two pieces. Or the undercut was extended three quarters of the way around so saw could be operated. Fallers worked with pride in making undercut which determined the direction the tree would fall. To test their accuracy, men would tap a stake in the ground where the tree was likely to fall and attempt to drop tree so it would drive stake in completely. Fallers spent

hours putting "razor edge" on double-bitted falling axes. With these keen edges and faller's skill, the surface of a good undercut would hardly show the mark of the blade. [Above] Falling 12-foot cedar in 1906 on Olympic Peninsula, with undercut completed and enough chips to fill a wagon. The girth of these big cedars was often too great for saw length. Their cores were generally rotten and it was then possible for the center to be hollowed out sufficiently for a faller to climb inside and operate one end of saw as it cut around thick shell. Instead of being wedged over, small charge of powder might be used to tip balance.

BUCKERS TAKE BREATHERS. [Above] Magnificent photograph of down cedar 16 feet in diameter at stump. Tree was bucked into five 32-foot logs which scaled 69,110 feet. [Right] Bucker starting work on a 12-foot cedar. This job was hard, lonely, tedious and bred men of patience and fortitude. Bucking, next to setting chokers on high lead and slack line rigging, was the most dangerous in the woods. Bucked logs easily rolled over when released from rest of tree and crushed workers. Buckers were also assailed by flying limbs from falling trees. Bottle hanging on bark is for oiling saw blade and demijohn on top of log is water jug.

There were big sawmills in every port—like Pope and Talbot operations at Port Ludlow—at Port Gamble, Port Madison, Port Blakely, Aberdeen, Bellingham, Seattle and Tacoma. Everywhere was the whush and whine of saws, harbors packed with booms of logs, sailing vessels waiting their turn to load. When the demand for lumber was extra heavy, ships were towed out of harbors with deck loads all but awash and masters' protests singing off the stays.

Mill hands, working in a roar of belts and the scream of saws, were paid $30 a month, room and board. And their brothers in the woods were swamping out new areas, cutting brush, cruising forest stands. Fallers were working on high springboards with axes as sharp as jackknives. Buckers were patiently pulling long crosscut saws through the green flesh of logs. Teams of oxen and horses were sweating and straining under the raucous oaths of punchers with goad

Bucker surveys two big firs lying beside stumps from which they were felled. Boss bucker was usually head of falling as well as bucking crews. Originally buckers worked in pairs but as practice of bucking "by the bushel," or piece work, came in they made more money and got along better by working alone.

and whip. Later logs were to be skidded faster by ground lead cables rigged to steam donkey engines.

At the turn of the century, many of the smaller companies were finding their best timber gone or difficult to log with limited capital and they began selling their holdings to the big outfits such as Merrill and Ring, Weyerhaeuser, Bloedel-Donovan, Schafer Brothers, Long-Bell and Simpson. However, there were many independent companies of large operations, such as Clear Lake Lumber Co. and the English companies.

The larger camps were well organized units of around two hundred men from woods boss to whistle punk. You had the Old Man — woods boss, camp superintendent or foreman, usually an old hand from Maine or Michigan. In the days of oxen, you had the bull whacker and teams of bulls brought from great distances to wrestle tons of weight down the skid roads. You had the punchers who spent their off hours nailing on shoes, two plates to each cloven hoof, repairing the slings which went under the bulls' bellies and yokes which locked their heads together. You had the skid road builder who laid out the roads, placed the hemlock cross and slough skids so the logs wouldn't hang up on them. He adzed out new skids and when they wore down, he mortised in pieces of maple.

When steam came in and spar trees went up,

(Continued on page 52)

Danger in the Woods

ACCIDENTS were continually happening in the woods and Darius Kinsey witnessed many of them, was a victim himself. Yet he refrained from photographing misery or any scene which would bring discredit upon the timber operators. He found some danger everywhere, exposed himself to it many times. But he took it in his stride as the loggers around him did. He was particularly careful about "side winders" or limbs and snags falling from nowhere and was always on guard.

Once a falling crew was working a thick mixed stand of huge, overripe timber. The cry of "Timber!" was sounded and every man jumped in the clear. The tree started down, falling true. One man was considerably behind it, supposedly in the safest spot of all. But the falling tree struck another with terrific force, felling it at a sharp angle; and this second tree broke off another, which in turn crashed down on the man who was farthest back from the cut.

In another case he was with three or four men on a windfall watching the last turn of logs come in. Fifty feet away a hemlock had been left intact. As the load drew near, something caught the haulback line, the load swung sharply toward the hemlock, and then crashed against it. The men on the windfall leaped for their lives, but one man's foot caught and he was crushed. No other load in the show had come anywhere near that lone hemlock.

Seven-foot Bloedel-Donovan log being bucked by cutting up from lower side after notching top side with axe. This was sometimes necessary to keep log from rolling on bucker or from pinching saw. Crosscut saws had demountable handles for use as either one or two-man. Buckers always kept bottle of saw oil handy.

BIGGEST SPRUCE. This 1925 spruce log was the largest Kinsey saw in his fifty years in the timber. Tree scaled 56,650 feet—a whole day's cut for many mills.

A big down fir in Sauk River Logging Co. near Darrington, Washington. Tree has been notched for bucking to 12-foot lengths.

Logger's Lament

THIS LETTER has been printed before in various forms and is reproduced here for color if not for fact.

"First I worked for a lumber company in the Hoh rain forest. This was back in 1900 and in those days did we have snow? We had to take our shovels to our bunks with us so as to be able to shovel our way out of the bunk house in the morning and it was so cold that when you spit out your tobacco cud you had to be careful not to spit on your foot for if you did it would bust your toe as the tobacco froze into solid ice before it hit the ground.

"At 4 in the morning the iron-headed old boss would stick his mug in the bunk house door and yell "Day light in the swamp" and the truth of it is it was two hours till daylight but that boss wasn't to be argued with and out we all rolled and got on our frozen boots and mukluks. We would all gang into the grub house at about 5 A. M. At 6 o'clock that same boss would yell "All out for the woods." We were already five miles deep in 'em. By daylight we would be arrived at our picnic ground and logging cedar out of the swamp. Along about noon the cook and his crew would show up with a flat log drawn by a horse with our pork and beans on it and we would brush the snow off the logs and sit down to eat in weather which was mostly around zero and I never have known since how good

Bucker ready to crosscut 10-foot fir. Smaller cedar in foreground was cut from a half buried windfall—a sound log even though on the ground more than a hundred years.

MAN'S STAND AGAINST NATURE. [Opposite] The Vanzer homestead in Washington's wilderness in 1906, perfect example of Kinsey's skill in taking full advantage of scanty natural light sifting down between canyons of trees. The estate was complete with outhouse utilizing hole formed by uplifted tree roots. Note extent of drifting smoke and clarity of objects even in the dimness of left ground. This photograph was reproduced in Life Magazine in 1951 to illustrate excellence of the work of early day operators. [Above] Cabin built of cedar slabs with bark left on. Shakes and inch-thick slabs were split from bolts with a froe, an iron splitting tool struck by wooden mallet—in limited use today. Note saw sharpening frame under lean-to.

pork and beans tasted and by the looks of the pork after careful examination I sometimes wonder if the hog wasn't boiled alive as I found many a hog's hair still growing on the rind but, it tasted mighty good anyway.

"At 4 o'clock which was about dark in the winter the boss would yell "All in." He didn't need to tell us that as we were sure all in by that time as that boss didn't give us time to take a decent breath all day and when you wanted to fill your pipe you had to get behind a tree so as the boss wouldn't see you but after you had it lit he didn't give a hoot. Well when we got back to camp at about 5 o'clock, as we had 2 or 3 miles to walk, we would wash up and get into the grub house at 6 sure and say, that coffee sure went good and it was so black you could of painted a boiler with it, and then some more pork and beans. I forgot to tell you that we had flapjacks for breakfast and they came in handy for other things too as we sometimes used them also for razor straps as no dern razor could cut them. After grub was over we would go back in the bunk house and

thaw out our boots and then take our shirts off and some of us after lighting up our old corncobs or taking a fresh chew of plug would play cards, some would play checkers, some would swap lies and say what glorious lies some of the old timers could tell, and the rest of us would keep busy searching for pa and ma greyback and the children and their grandpa and grandma. At 9 o'clock the geezer of a boss would come in and yell "Lights out" and then someone would blow out the lights of the two smoked up lanterns and we would all hit the hay and be ready to begin a bigger day tomorrow.

"Our one day was Sunday as we worked six days a week and washed our clothes and shaved and strapped our razors on dried flapjacks on Sundays. Pay day wasn't looked forward to because we didn't give a dang about money till spring as we had no way to spend it until we quit work in the spring, then many a fool lumberjack spent his whole winter's work by noon the first day in town. Ho hum! Some palmy days!"

there was the head rigger, in charge of hanging blocks and lines—the hook tender in the bull gang who bossed the choker men out where the trees were felled and bucked. If there was a railroad taking the logs out, it had an engineer and full crew. Every camp had a saw filer, a blacksmith, a carpenter, first and second cooks, bull cook and perhaps a fire patrol and speeder operator.

Here were bunkhouses, cook house, company store and blacksmith shop. And here was always a long day's work, eat, an hour or two at a card game in the kerosene lamp gloom and then deep sleep. No movies, no radio, no library—no wonder the food had to be good and abundant. If it

SHAKE CHALET. Brave little fruit trees enter life's struggle on this Olympic Peninsula stump ranch in 1906. Homesteaders in the new Northwest wrested meager livings from the forest by raising a few crops and cutting down trees as they needed them. Most homesteaders worked at logging or in sawmills leaving families to keep home fires burning between Sundays.

went down grade, so did the men, tin pants in their packs slung over their backs.

Four to six months in camp put bank rolls in the loggers' pockets even at the average pay of thirty to forty dollars a month, net after meals and clothing. Most of them were footloose bachelors, touchy as prima donnas, ready to pull up stakes at the first sign of unfair treatment. And

with hundred dollar bills wrapped around a chip, any good donkey puncher could skid himself to town and hang one on.

All this spelled industry to young Dee Kinsey. Here were people in colorful work and here was he with the tools of a livelihood, making photographic records of them. Better than picking hops with the Indians at a dollar a day or wres-

LOGGER PARTNERS [Opposite] find escape from flying chokers in this forest sanctuary. Walls were logs, roof built of long shakes, floor was dirt and silence profound. Light pattern and Kinsey's artistry make this a beautifully detailed photograph.

DEVIL'S CORNER [Above] This is the picture on the clock shelf of Sedro-Woolley home. Old prospector's trail on the north bank of Skagit River above Newhalem seen on road between George and Diablo power plants [Seattle City Light] on way to Ross Dam.

tling timbers on a sawmill green chain. But could he, a brash young fellow with a funny looking black box, get anywhere with these rough, roistering woodsmen?

He did because he saw beneath the logger's battered, brawling exterior, a simple, honest personality with the human yearning to perpetuate himself by photograph—a new and novel idea. All combed up, the fellow would be proud to send a picture of himself to his brother back in Minneapolis or Saginaw. Maybe he had a girl in town who would think of him oftener if she had there on the piano a constant reminder of her hero with his manly mustache flowing out over the teeth of a twelve-foot crosscut saw.

The first year of these junkets into the tall uncut was a story of trial and error, uncertain contact with the studio back to which every plate had to be sent for processing, many days wasted in traveling from camp to camp across rough mountain terrain. But Kinsey was serving his apprenticeship and building a fund of knowledge of the woods and his work.

By 1900 he was achieving his best results with the 20″ x 24″ Empire State View Camera manufactured by Rochester Optical Company. Operation of this monster would have instantly discouraged any present day cameraman. The plate holder alone, loaded with two standard polychrome glass plates, weighed over twenty-five pounds. And this camera had to be raised sometimes ten and twelve feet, for a true perspective of a tree with a swelling base. Such difficulties led Kinsey to smaller equipment—the 11″ x 14″ Eastman view camera with the high extension tripod.

A second camera in point of necessity was the Folmer and Schwing Cirkut camera which swung by clockwork on a circular track during exposure for panoramic effect. Views for stereoptican use were made with Rochester Optical's Stereoscopic Premo. Kinsey was continually experimenting with light and timing, developing and printing. However when he did strike a formula that satisfied him, he recognized its value and continued with it.

(Continued on page 65)

SUNDAY CONCERT. Forest pioneer fiddles for Kinsey in front of his early century estate. Shake cabin was temporary as backyard was filled with cabin logs. Note chimney from fireplace was also built of shakes lined with mud or clay.

WORLD'S FAIR LOG. Without a doubt the most famous log of the old Northwest logging days—diameter at stump, 16 feet and estimated at well over a thousand years old. Log attained fame as prize exhibit at Alaska Yukon Pacific Exposition in 1909 and remained on University of Washington campus for many years. Full length of log shown on opposite page

LOGGER ART. Group of wood carvings by Peter D. McMartin, pioneer logger of Stillaguamish area, about 1896. The figure of the woman was fashioned from a maple burl cut on the Potts claim at Hazel, Washington. A friend who worked with him, Ed Markwell, reports that McMartin later owned the Hazel Lumber Co., Lake Riley Lumber Co., and Apex Lumber Co. at Pe Ell, was a partner with Markwell and Joseph Irving in Security Logging Co. He was killed in a logging accident at French Creek. Many of the carvings are on display in Pioneer Clubhouse at Arlington, Washington.

A forerunner of logging arch. These wheels, ten feet high, were used to get lead end of logs off ground. One end of log was fastened under tongue; when oxen pulled, log would be lifted clear of ground permitting other end to be dragged more freely. Loggers shown are good specimens of rugged types bred by hard work and long hours.

WASHINGTON LANDMARK. Famous cedar was more than a thousand years old, 20 feet in diameter, when Kinsey photographed it first—opposite page top and bottom left. Later the tree was hollowed out to accommodate road and Kinsey drove his Ford into it, posing Mrs. Kinsey and son Darius by the car—opposite page bottom right. Still later the tree was sawed through at the ground, cut to 16 feet high and moved to U. S. Highway 99 near Silvana. This time Kinsey photographed his new Franklin with the stump —right. It remains beside the highway today, bearing the inscription: "Relic, A Vanquished Forest Western Red Cedar [Thuja Plicata Don] Age 1250 years. Preserved at Request of Snohomish County Pioneers, A. D. Arlington, Washington, 1922."

"THIS IS THE FOREST PRIMEVAL." Noble stand of Douglas fir at St. Paul and Tacoma's Nooksack Camp.

Kinsey caught the whole crew of one logging side in fine detail in this 1908 view. The picture shows transition in logging methods. Buckers, fallers and loading crews are posed on deck and carload of logs with donkey engine, line horse and Shay locomotive at left. Line on gin pole over heads of men in rear was rigged to donkey and used to roll logs from platform to cars.

Washington farmer and wife looking to the future from the top of one of their toothpicks—cedar log 52 feet in circumference.

OLDEST DONKEY. This is the original steam donkey designed by John Dolbeer of Dolbeer and Carson in Crescent City, California, and built by Murry Bros. in San Francisco. It was brought to the Grays Harbor woods by Alex Polson of Polson Logging Co., Aberdeen, Washington. The first boilers were built for 150 pounds working pressure with lap joint and burned slabs. This engine has been on display in Anderson Hall, University of Washington Forestry Building for many years. Gypsy or upright spool is shown with circular gear.

Engines in the Timber

STEAM and the donkey engine fully revolutionized logging. The Dolbeer donkey had an upright boiler which tapered into a stack with a single engine driving a vertical winch drum or spool from which the cable slack was pulled in hand over hand. A horse was used at first to pull the line out to the logs and became known as the "line horse."

Pacific Northwest engineering firms built many improvements into the early donkey engines—horizontal cylinders capable of transmitting tremendous power. Drums also became horizontal and haul back lines with big blocks and hooks were power-hauled out to the logs. The yarding method went like this. When the line got back to where the bucked logs were, perhaps 1000 feet or more, the hook tender jumped at the heavy block and pulled slack into the line, dropping the big hook over a choker, already looped around the log by the choker setters. He raised his hand and jumped clear. The "whistle punk" or boy who manned a whistle wire running back to the donkey, gave it a yank. At the signal, the donkey puncher pulled the lead line taut and then let in the steam. The engine roared and rocked on its skids as the line yanked the big log out of the brush. More steam and the log crashed, slashed, and pounded down the grade or out along the skid road, knocking down small trees willy nilly. With the line winding around the drum, the log thundered into the clear and hit the landing with a smashing thud.

Coupling turn of logs to endless cable connecting to landing donkey a mile down skid road. 1899 donkey in photograph is one of early types invented by John Dolbeer in 1885 which development eventually replaced the "hay burner" horse as skid road motive power. Note how skid road logs are worn from weight of skidded logs.

Instruction books and guide manuals were few and in themselves experimental. There were no exposure meters. Cameras were light proof but without refinement. A man simply made his own rules. Kinsey would get the image in focus on the ground glass and with full aperture, stop the lens down until proper dimness was reached, then cap the lens. After inserting plate holder, the lens cap was removed for length of exposure. In later years he used a Packard-type shutter.

The lens of the Eastman 11″ x 14″ was of Swiss manufacture equivalent to rapid rectilinear. Flashlight powders and accessories were so unsatisfactory, Kinsey used only well controlled natural light for interior shots which he avoided wherever possible. The first plates he used were far slower than some of the enlarging paper used today. In one of his early photos, two loggers who were standing in the background when the exposure was started, walked to the center foreground, turned around and sat down, to make a fair image on the plate.

Kinsey had his own method of taking photographs of big trees. It was sometimes an hour's work to arrange the camera at the proper height, distance and angle, even longer work to round up the people for the shot, perhaps waiting for them to finish the shift. A cedar tree, ten feet in diameter, splays out markedly at the ground. A camera shot at eye level would catch only the spreading base and would not depict the true shape of the tree. So it was usually necessary for Dee Kinsey to find a convenient stump twelve or so feet high, twenty or twenty-five feet away and by some herculean means get the big camera up on this natural platform. Often he had to build a makeshift scaffold or ladder to get an image free of distortion.

In the main the arrival of Darius Kinsey in camp was a welcome respite from the endless routine of board feet and sweat. He was a re-

DONKEY SERENADE. Wreck of 12 x 15 road donkey at N. C. L. Co.'s Camp 28 on June 9, 1911. Several of the crew were injured, the engineer killed.

Nine-foot fir log being hauled to landing slip by compound geared yarder. 1906 photograph shows how log landing was built. This ramp was 45 degrees.

freshing breeze from the outside world—friendly, quick-witted, an entertaining talker in the bunkhouse. An illustration is given by a Seattle business man of today, Palmer Lewis, who recounts that "Kinsey was charged with a contagious enthusiasm that made you feel important to be photographed by him. He was allowed around any of the operations. I was running a company speeder on the railroad out of a camp and had strict orders to allow no riders. One summer we were harassed by forest fires and another itinerant photographer had got into the timber without authorization from our testy woods boss. After taking some pictures he made the mistake of his life by trying to sell some in camp. The Old Man let out a blast that nearly blew the fellow out of camp. He said he saw enough fires without having to look at pictures of them. He

had this poor chap headed down the track on foot before he could collect his senses."

For many years Kinsey interspersed his own activities with assignments for the Seattle, Lake Shore and Eastern Railroad of which he was official photographer and J. Hamilton Lewis was attorney. However these were pictures of the mountains and timber right in the line of his other work and did not take him far afield. He also made many views for the Great Northern Railway Co. and subsidiaries, Willmar and Sioux Falls Railway Co. and Montana Central Railway Co. A newspaper notice of the time stated:

"D. R. Kinsey of the firm of Kinsey & Kinsey, of Snoqualmie, Washington, official artists for the Seattle, Lake Shore & Eastern Railway company, arrived last Tuesday night. He is here in the interest of his firm, taking logging views,

Yarding and loading in 1908. Donkey engine at left is yarder which has just dragged a 10-foot fir log 600 feet on ground to the landing. Railroad cars are in front of gin pole used for loading by second donkey.

views of big trees, etc., and exhibiting many handsome specimens of their work, most of which were taken along the line of the above named road. The object of his visit here is to take views from this section to be used by the railroad company in advertising in the east and showing some of the interesting features of the leading industry of Puget Sound. Mr. Kinsey spent some time along the Peninsular railway, and yesterday afternoon he went up the line of the Shelton Southwestern road, and from there he will visit Simpson's camps on the Kamilche road and will return here in about ten days."

With the rapid development of the new country, Dee Kinsey had many temptations that meant good money and less hardship for himself and family. In 1897 the steamer "Portland" had tied up in Seattle with the first gold from the Klondike and the following year the big rush was on. With the riches flowing in and out of the city, opportunities for a good photographer were endless. The hotels were jammed to overflowing, people slept in tents and woodsheds, money was spent freely as the cries went out that there was plenty more of its kind in Alaska.

The Navy Yard was established in Bremerton, the city of Seattle dredged the Duwamish River for ocean going vessels, the Alaska-Yukon-Pacific Exposition in 1909, the launching of the $100,000 ferry "Clallam" and its placing on the

One of the first steam yarding units to go into the woods was the upright gypsy type shown in this 1898 view. The line was pulled back into the woods by a line horse and three or four wraps were taken around the "spool." When the log had been attached to the hauling line, it was hauled down the skid road.

Who is This Fellow...
The Logger?

"THE LOGGER," said George M Cornwall, lumber publication executive for many years, in his address to the 1932 Pacific Logging Congress, "is a natural born engineer, resourceful and patient He likes new ideas but is not overly prone to adopt new methods until they have been tested by actual performance. He likes to "tinker" with new machines. If the equipment breaks down he calls to his assistance the shop mechanic or the "donkey doctor." He will struggle along until he gets the machine going again. Hours mean nothing to a logger while repairing a break down, be it either a bridge destroyed by flood, slide or fire; a donkey gone "haywire," or a locomotive in the ditch. It is all in the day's work, and the logs must be kept moving to the sawmill.

"The professionally trained engineer has a somewhat different mental attitude toward the industry and life than the hardy pioneer logger of California, Oregon, Washington, Idaho, Montana, Arizona, New Mexico, Colorado, South Dakota, and British Columbia, who started his logging career where the outfit consisted of a jackscrew, a single-bitted axe and a few wedges, supplemented in other camps with a piece of manila rope, a handful of small blocks and an ox team. But with this primitive equipment logs were rolled into the streams and floated on the freshets to the mills.

"The men who constitute the crews of the average logging camp usually include various nationalities — American, Canadian, English, Scotch, Irish, Danish, Norwegian, Swedish, Finnish, Russian, German, Austrian, Greek, Italian and Japanese. The latter three nationalities confine their activities chiefly to road construction and track maintenance. From the contact of these varied races springs a wealth of cosmopolitan ideas. In the average bunkhouse one will get a good cross-section of the world's thought. Men from all ranks of life seem to gravitate to the logging camps. One will often find men with classical educations — lawyers, doctors, teachers and men who have held important positions — tucked away in some relatively obscure camp, who will surprise you with their profound knowledge of various subjects. The logger likes to read. The daily newspaper and the radio keep him in close touch with the world's events. He is a born sport. Baseball, horse racing, football and boxing have a keen interest for him. He will back his judgment with his last dollar.

"In politics and religion he is a free lance. His religious ideas may be summed up in the thought expressed by Paine: 'The world is my country, and to do good is my religion.' He brings into the discussion of nearly every economic and political question the background of experience gained in the country in which he was born, as well as other countries in which he has traveled.

"The early logging crews on the Pacific Coast consisted principally of state of Mainers, and "bluenoses" from Nova Scotia, who came around the Horn in sailing ships. Sailors who deserted their ships became loggers and their knowledge of handling rigging came into mighty good play. Later, the lumberjacks of Michigan, Wisconsin and Minnesota rolled their blankets and trekked to the tall timber belts of the Pacific Greater West and helped lay the foundation of this mighty logging industry. We revere the memories of these early logging men."

Yarding donkey using turntable. The circular bottom frame was built so that engine would be turned to direction of incoming logs. The plan was not successful as line would not lead on the drum. The manufacturers used second drum to haul line back but with circular frame it was difficult to work line in. The method found best was to run line through block at end of sled.

run between Port Angeles, across the Straits of Juan de Fuca, to Victoria, B. C.—all these set up glittering pressures in Darius Kinsey to take news pictures and sell copies of them all over the world. But Dee had chosen the woods for his life and the men who pulled the long stroke on the bucker's crosscut saw and swung the wide arc with double-bitted axes, were his love and livelihood. The woods won as they always did when he was tempted into other fields, and they repaid him mightily for his faithfulness.

As Darius Kinsey was cutting his niche in the lumber industry, many lumber fortunes were being founded in Grays Harbor and the Olympic Peninsula Kinsey took pictures in some of these camps. Peter, Hubert and Albert Schafer started

logging with oxen in 1893, later with steam donkeys, driving logs down the Satsop River into the Chehalis to Aberdeen. In 1915 they changed to high lead and duplex loader methods; operating 100 miles of railroad at one time, with 8 locomotives and 315 log cars. J. A. Morley of Saginaw, Michigan, organized the Saginaw Timber Co. in 1896. Henry McCleary built a sawmill, shingle mill and sash and door plant, naming the town McCleary, with a railroad into the Black Hills.

Capt. A. M. Simpson started the first sawmills on Grays and Willapa Harbor, Washington; Coos Bay and Port Orford, Oregon, and operated a redwood mill in California, another sawmill on

(Continued on page 76)

Top quality spruce in Puget Sound Mills and Timber Co. operation near Port Angeles—cut from tree which scaled 37,000 feet. [Below] Looking down skid road toward yarding donkey. Pulley mounted on stump carried endless cable. This photograph is believed to have been taken in Snoqualmie Valley. Northwestern Lumber Co. operated near here, owned by Horton and Barclay of Pennsylvania. North Bend Lumber Co. logged in this general area—Webb Vinnage, manager, and George Reck, foreman.

MAIN LINE SKID ROAD. Near top of main line skid road showing well worn cross logs. Hemlock was generally used for its comparative hardness. There is depth and detail in every chip and sliver in this photograph—even to the spiraled wires in cable running over snubbing drum. Line at right over man's arms is in motion. Road donkey 500 feet up slope.

Log Detectives

THE JOB of recovering lost and stolen logs was a necessary part of the industry in logging's heyday. Logs were always somebody's property and the brand hammered into the butt by iron shapes, proclaimed the fact. Yet they were pilfered by beach combers or log pirates or washed out of booms and rafts by high waters and tides.

Log patrols were first organized by loggers and sawmill men in Grays Harbor in 1923 when lost, strayed or stolen logs were costing them $100,000 a year. The following year the Port Gardner patrol was started in the Everett area, and in 1925 lumber firms in the Bellingham, Anacortes and Blaine districts were rounding up their own logs. By 1928 the Tacoma-Shelton-Olympia area was being similarly patrolled.

Operation of the log patrol usually began with the report of logs missing by tug boat operators or boom men—even waterfront residents. Patrols operated speed boats that scouted bays and inlets, and enlisted the services of small tug boat owners who eventually located most of the logs and towed them to a log pool. Logs were sold and records kept according to the owners' butt brands; charges for the service being made to each firm involved.

The same condition existed as in the salmon industry. A few independent and unscrupulous mills made a practice of buying contraband logs at cut prices and pirates deliberately stole them to supply the demand. At one time twelve sawmills between Ballard and Deception Pass kept busy on stolen logs alone. The thieves would wait for favorable night tides, slip up to an unguarded log tow, uncouple the last section, let the logs drift free and round them up later. Original brands were cut off in the ponds and the logs were rebranded. One delivery of stolen logs scaled 200,000 feet.

The log patrols hired operatives who joined with the log thieves and beachcombers, learned how they operated and to whom they sold logs. This spy system in one case turned up several county officials who were being paid off by the pirates for tips on log raft movements.

In time, through the efficient operation of the various log patrols, laws were revised, strict regulations enforced, heavier protection set on log rafts and illicit sawmills put out of business. The business of stealing logs has long been a thing of the past although big lumber operators still employ scouts to round up wayward logs.

[Above] Trouble on the line in 1910. Log being skidded on ground has apparently wedged itself into a windfall. Detail shows sniped end of log and butt rigging. Line around log is choker. [Below] Spruce logging at Puget Sound Mill and Timber Co., Port Angeles, showing second type donkey engine in Washington woods, made by Washington Iron Works in 1890. The original was a single drum 9 x 10 engine but the one in this photo was altered with the addition of haulback drum for leading line back into the woods. This lumber firm was organized in 1890 by Mike Earles who built narrow gauge railroad west of Port Angeles. Ed Gerrens was manager.

Tacoma compound-geared yarder taking logs up the skid road Due to the fact that the straight geared engine used ¾" to ⅞" line, a good many of the logs had to be blocked. By this method, a block was fastened to the choker on the logs and the line fastened to a convenient stump. Sometimes the choker would have to be rolled to change the angle of pull on the log so it could be moved past an obstruction such as a stump.

Logging Chance

BEFORE big timber operators logged an area they sent out "cruisers" whose job it was to survey the trees for quality and density, "lay of the land," burns and barrens, gulleys and streams. The woods superintendent then laid his campaign for getting the timber out the quickest and most economical way. That was the "logging chance."

Usually the best chance was taken first, always with an eye to the next one and the rise and fall of the lumber market. It was not necessarily true that logs cost more the deeper the railroad went into the woods or the farther from headquarters the camps were placed. The biggest logs might lie the highest and farthest away, and generally the biggest logs were the most profitable.

The cruiser was an expert with compass, tape line and log scale. He usually had an assistant who could cook and the two packed their way into the virgin timber, cruising it systematically back and forth, across and through until they had accurate figures of footage and topographical maps of the whole area. The pair might be gone two weeks or a month but they brought back data with which the woods boss could judge the chance. He might not be satisfied with one cruising, perhaps not with six, but in the end he could start surveying for his log transportation, the key to every logging operation.

Roads or railroads had to be built so they could be lengthened, and from which connecting roads could reach into all areas to be logged. All the time these roads must be going up, so the loads on trucks or railroad cars could be hauled down. Trestles and bridges had to be built and yarding lanes laid out on the maps. Sites for camps had to be selected. Not until all these plans were made and drawn, did the logging operator know whether or not he had a good logging chance.

Logs on ground lead dogged together and yarded by Washington Iron Works 10 x 12 road engine.

the Columbia River—the latter subsequently owned by P. J. Brix. The Willapa Harbor mill at South Bend was purchased by Ed Gaudette.

Al Coats and Senator J. E. Fordney of Michigan, were partners in Coats-Fordney Lumber Co. operating on Wishkah River. Ben Johnson was manager. Property was sold to Donovan Corkery in 1924. Wynoochee Timber Co. was also active, owned by Gus Carlson, Bert Callow and Frank Lamb, whose firm Lamb-Grays Harbor Co. was an important manufacturer of logging blocks. Schafer Bros. later acquired the operation. Other loggers were Peter Connacher, Peter Klein, and Tom Soule.

Sol G. Simpson started the Simpson Logging Co. in 1895 which has operated continuously in the Shelton area for almost 60 years. Mark Reed, Simpson's son-in-law became president of the company after the death of A. H. Anderson in 1914 who succeeded to the office after Simpson died in 1906. Prior to this Reed had been manager of the Mercantile Co., Simpson Logging Co. and Peninsular Railway. He was virtually in charge of all Simpson interests, the railroad then having 50 miles of track.

D. E. Skinner was president of Port Blakely Mill in Kitsap County. John and Jim Eddy were associated with him in this enterprise. The Mason County Logging Co., operated by the Bordeaux brothers, owned the Mason County Railroad and a mill at Bordeaux. Joseph Vance built a mill at Malone and his own railroad into

(Continued on page 93)

[Opposite page, top] Shingle mill at end of 3-mile flume which carried stream of water 40 feet high, paralleling mountain stream. Photo at bottom left shows section of flume. Next 1100 cords of shingle bolts in pond at mill with old skid road. [Above] Strapped bundles of shingles entering and leaving dry kiln of McMaster Lumber and Shingle Co. [Below] Another view of shingle mill and flume.

Small sawmills like these sprang up in every community near the timber and were abandoned as the cut ran out. They were "circular" mills using one circular head saw from 30" to 48" in diameter for ripping logs with one or more cut-off saws for cutting boards to length. Product was rough, not planed or sanded unless sent to planing mills. Photo below shows stump rancher bringing in logs to be converted into family flour and beans.

FAMILY ENTERPRISE. Small shingle mills like this one of Rayment Shingle Co. in Port Angeles, Washington in 1919, were a vital part of community economy. In small settlements men, women and children made shingles out of the cedar bolts and missing fingers proved it. Loggers and sawmill workers held themselves a class or two above and to call a man a "shingle weaver" was as good as inviting a fight.

Pleasure boats like this were used on larger lakes in Washington forty years ago, such as Lake Whatcom near Bellingham. The Larson mill on Lake Whatcom had pioneered this area and was taken over by Bloedel-Donovan who had built Bellingham Bay and British Columbia Railroad as a logging road and converted it later to a common carrier In 1921 on Olympic Peninsula, J. J. Donovan who had acquired timber from New York interests, bought Goodyear Lumber Co. at Clallam Bay and made connections with Port Angeles and Western Railroad at Sekiu. From here logs made into Davis rafts were towed to Bellingham.

Shingle mill interior showing bolts entering on conveyor. Battery of twelve saws is in motion at right. Shingles dropped to endless belt on lower level. [Below] Allen-Nelson sawmill at Monohon on Lake Samammish near Seattle—typical of medium-sized mill, usually identified by screened dome of refuse burner, prime source of power. Company boarding house and cabins shown against hill behind planing mill. Many of these mills ran day and night and inspired the poetical line—"The day shift works at labor but the night shift weaves romance."

Tidewater mill at Port Gamble, Washington. [Below] Mountain view of Clear Lake mill and town in 1906. Mill produced 100 million feet of lumber and 200 million shingles annually at peak of production.

FROM DOCK TO DECK. Three types of lumber carriers at dock of Crown Lumber Co., Mukilteo, Washington, on Puget Sound. Ship at left is Nelson Line freighter running to East Coast. Ship in middle is coastwise lumber steamer. Four-

masted schooner at right In the days of plenty, ships had
brisk trade in Pacific Northwest woods and carried loads
chained to the deck which were often washed overboard.
Much lumber is still exported from larger ports in this region

TIMBER AT TIDEWATER. Logs for sawmills on Puget Sound are towed in rafts and stored in booms at millside. Wearing "corked" boots and wielding pikepoles, boom men sort out logs and maneuver them to chain lifts. Lumber stowed on barges is for short water hauls. Ship cargo is for East Coast, California or foreign ports. [Photo above] Port Gamble Mill in 1906.

Windjammers at Lumber Dock

ONE of the most unique lumber carriers was the seven-mast iron barkentine *E. R. Sterling*, built in Belfast in 1883 and launched as the *Columbia* for German owners. About 1907 the vessel was wrecked off the Washington coast but was salvaged, admitted to American register and rebuilt as a seven master, with square sails on her foremast. Her unusual rig attracted attention in every port. For many years she carried lumber, 2,500,000 feet per voyage, from North Pacific to Australia, usually returning with coal. About 1927 she was damaged in a North Atlantic hurricane. Towed to a port in the United Kingdom, she was scrapped. Other large-carrying sailers were several of the Dollar fleet, most of them previously German-owned and war-captured. The *Alexander Dollar* and some of the others carried

3,000,000 feet or more. Of the large wooden carriers the *Oregon Fir* and *Oregon Pine*, five-masters, built on the Columbia in 1920, had a capacity of 2,400,000 feet.

Loading of lumber was done either by chutes extending over bow or stern or through stern ports, boards poked a few at a time. Cargoes usually ran from 250,000 to 500,000 feet. In earlier times the captains served as sales managers and many cargoes left the Pacific Coast unsold, the skipper driving the best bargain he could on making port.

Until World War II, the schooners *Commodore*, built at Seattle in 1919, and *Vigilant*, built at Hoquiam in 1920, were regularly engaged in the lumber carrying trade between North Pacific ports and the Hawaiian Islands for the firms of Lewers & Cooke and City Mill Co. The *Commodore* carried 1,500,000 feet, and the *Vigilant* 1,700,000 feet. The last of the larger windjammers engaged in active deep sea service, they freighted many cargoes to the Islands, keen rivalry existing between masters and crews. The *Commodore's* last voyage from this coast was to South Africa during the war. She was then reported engaged in coasting trade in that country. The *Vigilant* was sailed by Capt.

Head saw and carriage of Snoqualmie Falls Lumber Co. Big log stands at end of cut, with band saw showing over sawyer's right shoulder. Saws in big mills ranged from 12 to 16 inches wide, 40 to 50 feet in endless band, sometimes "double-cut" with teeth on each edge to saw log as carriage moved back and forth. Saws were sent to filing room for sharpening twice a day and the filers had highly important work. Power for saws and other machinery was usually derived from burning slab and sawdust waste—now slabs are sold for fuel and big mills operate by purchased electricity. Sawyers were and are the "golden boys" of the mills, highly paid, vital to production and profit. Setters rode carriage and regulated width of cut.

One of the larger and best known sawmills in the State of Washington—plant of Snoqualmie Falls Lumber Co. at Snoqualmie. Mill was built in 1916 by Weyerhaeuser interests and managed by Mr. Warren with Cutler Lewis as logging superintendent. Has been in full operation ever since. Main source of logs for the mill was in the Cascade Mountains in the area drained by South, Middle and North forks of Snoqualmie River. Lower view shows same log as on opposite page with six-foot slabs on way to trimmers and edgers.

Matt Peasley, famous character in Peter B. Kyne's lumber stories.

There was also the *Alice Cooke,* built at Port Blakely in 1891, the predecessor of the *Commodore.* For years the *Cooke* plied the route between North Pacific ports and the islands almost as regularly as a steamer, carrying 900,000 feet each voyage. She was finally withdrawn and replaced by the larger *Commodore.* The schooner, built at Port Blakely in 1889, operated with the *Alice Cooke.*

In addition to the *Commodore* and *Vigilant,* other well known sailers built from 1918 to 1920 for lumber

carrying included the *Betsy Ross, Ecola, K. V. Kruse, L. W. Ostrander, Malahat, Monitor, North Bend, Oregon Fir, Oregon Pine, S. P. Tolmie, George U. Hind, Fort Laramie, Ella A., Elinore H., Forest Dream, Forest Friend, Forest Pride, Conqueror, Anne Comyn, Katherine MacKall* and many others which have outlived their usefulness. Few of these vessels made profit for their owners as they were caught in the post-war depression and the competition of steam.

The steam schooner was a type developed on and peculiar to the North Pacific. It was designed for the rapid handling of lumber. Many of the early carriers

[Above] Fifty feet high and still growing. 1928 view of lumber stacks in yard of Seattle Cedar Lumber Manufacturing Co.'s yard. Company was founded in 1890 by A. F. McEwan. Hilke Piler at left is standard in industry—invented by Company's late general superintendent for many years. Standing figure in front of tractor is Sigurd Stevens, present yard foreman.

[Opposite page] One of Darius Kinsey's finest for profound depth and detail. This photograph could be enlarged to six or eight feet high without losing proper form and texture. Fallers have finished undercut, would next saw half way through from back of tree, drive in steel wedges to keep blade free. Minutes before tree was to fall, man with stoutest lungs would bellow "Timber-r-r-r!" to warn buckers and men cutting slash. Crash would be deafening. Expert fallers could "lay a tree on a dime" or drive a stake into the ground.

were "single enders" because they had engines and housing aft thus affording an entire sweep of the deck, unobstructed and clear for long lengths, permitting speed in both loading and discharge. In those days a carrier of 500,000 feet was in the large class. However, experience prompted still larger vessels until average capacity rose to 1,000,000 feet and later to 1,500,000 feet. Many were especially designed for carrying long lengths on deck. Plans for the typical steam schooner provided for ample stability with about two-fifths of the cargo in the hold, three-fifths as a deck load. Consequently these handy, useful craft looked like floating lumber stacks when outward bound. One fact that

prompted the single-ended type was the fact that in the smaller ports, many of them shallow, the carrier had to nose into a pier. With machinery aft, the bow rode high and thus it was possible to reach berths that vessels on even keel could not serve. The steam schooners also carried long wooden booms, 70 to 75 feet in length, so that they could reach to the end of the loading dock and thus eliminate labor and moving berth. Fast handling was attained by a winch with off-shore and inshore falls, operated by one driver. The double enders later were equipped with fast gear both fore and aft, some of them with runways through the midship house permitting deck loading of long lengths.

[Left] Caterpillar tractor No. 1881, owned by Monroe Mill Co., had plenty of power to drag sleds of shingle bolts along rough ground. Small logs in middle of road kept skids in line. [Below] More detailed view of 1881 was taken April 27, 1915. This was Model 60, manufactured about 1912 at Stockton, California. Machine had valve-in-head engine, four cylinders, 550 rpm, two speeds forward, one reverse.

Tractors in the Timber

ONE of the first crawler tractors to enter Pacific Northwest logging was the small Cletrac used by Schafer Bros. Logging Co. in its Grays Harbor operations. Another early model was the McCormick-Deering TracTractor — one of these, the T-40, was used by Knutsen Bros. at Husum, Washington. The first International crawler was the T-20 built in 1931. In contrast

[Above left] Shingle bolts on way to mill by Fordson farm tractor converted to narrow gauge railroad oper ated by Bloedel-Donovan bolt camp of which Charlie Brown was superintendent. Horses dragged the loaded sleds to railside. Tractor had sand "boxes" and hoses in front of wheels. [Above right] Saddle-back "lokey" getting shingle bolts out of woods. [Below] Close-up of Skagit MAC "side rod" locomotive used in Bloedel-Donovan operation above, without sanding units.

is the big TD-24, 6 cyl. diesel—182″ long and weighing 36,275 pounds. The Oliver-Cletrac FDC was a large 6 cyl. diesel logging tractor with 26,800 pound pull in low, 26,900 in reverse.

As early as 1921 Caterpillar tractors were ground hauling logs at Mendocino Lumber Co. in California. The Cat D8 now weighs 34,600 pounds, is 6 cyl. diesel

with speed from as high as 4.8 mph in forward high to 3.7 mph in reverse high.

Allis-Chalmers had an early model in the L0 which went into service at the Hammond and Little River Redwood Co., Crannell, California, in 1935. The 40,000 pound HD-19 Allis Chalmers has hydraulic torque converter and hydraulic steering

SOLDIERS IN THE SPRUCE. Highlight of World War I in the big woods was assignment of battalions of soldiers to log the spruce needed in building airplanes. [Opposite, above] Soldier loggers on Sultan Railway and Timber Co. property, July 1918. Early logger in this area was George Startup for whom town was named. [Below] Loyal legions of loggers who bought Liberty Bonds at Camp 9, Lyman Timber Co., Hamilton, Washington. Photos on wall at left are Darius Kinsey's—one at upper right [the bull team] shown on page 21 of this book.

these hills, later expanding into other enterprises as the Vance Lumber Co.

Frank Fredson logged in Mason County in the '90's and had his own railroad in 1920. J. H. Izett built a road in from Brinnon on Hood Canal, using geared locomotives.

In 1912 George Webb, an English sailor who had logged the area where Fauntleroy in West Seattle is now, bought timber on Snow Creek on Olympic Peninsula and with Jim Sobey built a logging road. Later they built another road up the Duckabush River.

One well known bull team logger in the Puget Sound area was Charles Clemmons, who with his father had arrived from Maine. About 1900 Charles Clemmons acquired timber on Chehalis River and built a railroad into timber, Carl Wiecks logging boss. This property was taken over by Weyerhaeuser Timber Co. for a tree farm which Frank Byles managed for many years.

Lou Olson operated on White River with a mill at Enumclaw. Theodore F. Peterman had a big sash and door factory in Tacoma to which his son, Al, added a plywood factory, inventing and building motor trucks and trailers.

During these years, Robert Dollar exported lumber to China, Pat McCoy had timber holdings in Washington and British Columbia, J. P. Brix logged on the Columbia River as did O. M. Clark.

Long-Bell Lumber Company built one of the biggest sawmills in the world and established the town of Longview, Washington. J. D. Tennant was manager of the mill. In the early 1900s, Lloyd Crosby was bridge builder on Peninsular Railroad and became chief timber cruiser for George S. Long, Sr., pioneer lumberman and general manager of Weyerhaeuser Timber Co., was later promoted to engineer in charge of building the Weyerhaeuser road from South Bay up Skookum Chuck to Vail, where Ronald McDonald was logging manager. Al Raught, Ed Baker, and Walter Ryan were well known Weyerhaeuser employees in the early days. Crosby went to Klamath Falls, Oregon, and built a logging road from the new Weyerhaeuser pine mill into Cascade timber. When Consolidated Timber Co. was formed in Portland to salvage the Tillamook Burn, he was made manager. In Long-Bell's southern Washington operations, Bill Ryder, who hailed from Bogalusa, La., invented the "long car" for logging. The

(Continued on page 99)

HOMES IN THE HILLS. When railroads came into the woods, the logger's standard of living went up and most of the color went out. Logging was a business, highly competitive and requiring full efficiency of operation. Logging camps did not "follow the timber" but remained as permanent bases from which railroad spurs branched out like curving tentacles to five or six "sides." Large buildings in each of these three photos are cook houses with shops and store houses near them. Other buildings were loggers' living quarters. [Above, opposite] Bloedel-Donovan Calawa Camp. Bunkhouses were built to be loaded on rail cars and moved to next camp.

VICTUALS UP! Cook sounding dinner call at typical logging camp—wielding "gut hammer" on iron triangle. Loggers were fed like prima donnas with heavy, solid foods that included three or four kinds of meat at every meal. Cooks, called "gut robbers," were highly paid and highly criticized no matter how well they fed the crews. Tables were kept set at all times and men had numbered places, ate until they were full. Disconnected trucks on track are lined up ready for trip back to woods.

Logging camps and sawmills were the main support of families outside the Puget Sound and Pacific Coast cities. A man from Minnesota got a stump farm for next to nothing and got less than that for what he could raise. He whacked together a one-room shake house and barn and perhaps planted an apple or pear orchard. He went to work in the woods and came home when he could while his wife and children raised vegetables, and cut the hay. On Sundays or when the log camp was shut down on account of snow or forest fires, he shot a deer or elk and did his own logging at home. Falling and bucking trees he could handle, he got them loaded on the makeshift wagon and hauled them to the nearest saw or shingle mill.

Photo below is Vail, headquarters camp of Weyerhaeuser Timber Co. in June, 1938. Weyerhaeuser Timber Co. operations are still the largest in the world. Logging at Vail supplied the company's million-foot mills at Everett. Shipped by train 30 miles to South Bay on Puget Sound, logs were rafted to Everett. Company operated Oregon facilities at Klamath Falls, and in Washington in Grays Harbor, Olympia, Snoqualmie River area— mills at Enumclaw and Raymond.

The big logging camps and many of the larger inland mills took great pride in the "tables they set." Darius Kinsey ate at such dining rooms as this where the tables groaned with food, the men crowding in and staggering out. One incident is recalled where a logger tripped and fell in the dinner gong stampede. When he picked himself up he looked chagrined and started back to the bunkhouse, mumbling, "No use goin' to dinner now. Won't be anything left."

Combination dining room and kitchen in large Washington logging camp. Cups were big and saucers deep and wide for blowing and slurping.

Contribution of J. I. Case Co. to log hauling in the big woods was this steam logging engine which found limited utility about 1907. It carried big boxes of fuel on each side of driver but had to have handy source of slab on its route.

REVERIE. Man seems lost in the great spaciousness of eternity as sunbeams filter through shadow-draped trees to ferns and down log. Darius Kinsey made this artistic photograph in 1911.

town of Ryderwood was Long-Bell's Pacific County headquarters.

The records in the Kinsey collection do not list all the logging firms in whose camps Darius Kinsey took photographs but the following names are identified with negatives or prints:

English Logging Company Camps—Nos. 9-10-11.

Bloedel-Donovan Lumber Mills—*Calawa, Sekiu, Sappho, Alger, Beaver, Skykomish, Saxon, Silvana, Delvin Camps*

Lyman Timber Co.

Alpine Logging Co.

Florence Logging Co.—*Monroe*

Allen-McRae—*Glacier*

Merrill and Ring—Camp 4

Crescent-Piedmont Logging Co.

Day Lumber Co.

Wallace Falls Timber Co.—*Gold Bar*

Snoqualmie Falls Lumber Co.—Camp A

Snow Creek Logging Co.—*Blyn*

Cherry Valley Timber Co.—*Stillwater*

Hama Hama Logging Co.

Chas. R. McCormick—*Port Gamble*

Sound Timber Logging Co.—*Darrington*

Admiralty Logging Co.—*Edmonds*

Siler Logging Co.

Florence Logging Co.—*Maltby*

Raymond Timber Co.

St. Paul and Tacoma Lumber Co.—*Nooksack*

Sauk River Logging Co.

Eagle Logging Co.

Wickersham Logging Co.

Weyerhaeuser Timber Co.—*Vail*

Skagit Mill Co.

UNSUNG HEROES OF THE WOODS. Vital tools of fallers and buckers were the crosscut saws and they had to be kept sharp, straight and clean by hand setting, swaging, and filing, the kinks hammered out. Filers were a race by themselves, highly skilled, usually modest. They were cultivated by "crosscut demonstrators" employed by saw makers such as Simonds, Disston and Atkins who traveled from camp to camp, living and working with the men.

Wayland Mill Co.
Puget Sound Pulp and Timber—*Clear Lake*
Washington Pulp and Paper Co —*Sail River*
Crown-Willamette Co.
Everett Logging Co.
Webb Logging Co.—*Brinnon*
West Fork Logging Co.— *Bremerton*
Miller Logging Co.
Clausen and Olesen—*Sekiu*
Phoenix Logging Co.—*Potlatch*
Androus Logging Co.—*Darrington*
Canyon Creek Logging Co.—*Granite Falls*
Ebey Logging Co.
Dempsey Logging Co.—*Lyman*
Crown Logging Co.
O. H. Clemons—*Montborn*
E. H. Lester—*Montesano*
Sultan Railway and Timber Co.—*Oso*
Eagle Falls Timber Co.
Hutchinson Creek Shingle Co.—*Acme*
Lamson Logging Co.—*Darrington*

Polson Logging Co.—*Hoquiam*
Bork Brothers Logging Co.
Lake Riley Lumber Co.—*Hazel*
Imperial Fir Lumber Co.—*Lynden*
Rasor Brothers—*Granite Falls*
Knutson-Nelson—*Skykomish*
Stimson Lumber Co.—*Camp Belfair*
Hoff and Pinkey—*Deming*
Klenert and Kennedy—*Fortson*
Clear Lake Lumber Co.
Lake Grandy Timber Co.
Newcomb Shingle Co.—*Blaine*
Hanken Lumber Co.—*Sedro-Woolley*
Winklers Camp—*Birdsview*
Ozark Lumber Co.
Security Logging Co.—*Alpine*
Fidalgo Lumber and Box Co.—*Anacortes*
Woodinville Shingle Co.
North Bend Timber Co.
Monroe Shingle Co.
Puget Sound Mill and Timber—*Port Angeles*
Arlington Mill Co.

McCleary Mill Co.
Wood and Knight
Seattle Cedar Lumber Mfg. Co.
West Fork Logging Co. *Bremerton*
Simmons Shingle Co.—*Stillwater*
Snohomish River Boom Co.
Waite Mill and Timber—*Granite Falls*
Stephens-Bird—*Monroe*
Faber Logging Co.
Erickson Shingle—*Marysville*
Loth Shingle Co.—*Granite Falls*
Marone Mill Co.—*Acme*
Eclipse Mill Co.—*Everett*
Hardwood Products—*Sedro-Woolley*
Modern Shingle Co.—*Edmonds*
Getchell Mill Co.
Raymond Lumber Co.—*Raymond*
Rucker Brothers—*Everett*
Lewis and Mowat
Blue Mountain Logging Co.
Washington Lumber and Spar Co.—*Renton*
Rayment Shingle Co.—*Port Angeles*
Wisconsin Timber Co.—*Stanwood*
Bolcom-Canal Lumber Co.
Wood-Acme Logging Co.—*Acme*
Pacific States Lumber Co.—*Selleck*
McDonald and Peterson—*Deming*
Elbe Logging Co.—*Elbe*
Bryan and Reed—*Arlington*
Bergin and Co.
Forks Logging Co.
Allen-Nelson Mill Co.—*Lake Samamish*
Maine Logging Co.
McNeil and O'Hearn

Sawmill and logging towns at the turn of the century had many saloons and dance halls which preyed on the loggers' thirst for drinks and adventure. They were social clearing houses for him and his kind, or places for "shows" and wild revelry. From there lumberjacks flocked through the swinging doors of ornate saloons into the tense hum of magnificent gambling houses, or to dance halls where painted ladies waited. Everywhere on his skidroad the lumberjack was in his own element. He met his friends from everywhere, their faces brightened with pleasure instead of being grimy, drawn and weary with toil.

Colorful in this manner was the old Humboldt, in Aberdeen, described so vividly by James

(Continued on page 112)

"Fire in the Timber!"

AN ever-present menace to Darius Kinsey's livelihood, at once tragedy and bitter frustration to the men who owned and cut timber, was the forest fire. When the temperature went up and humidity down, the woods got crackling dry. A fisherman's campfire would run down a dead tree root, smolder for days and eventually the snag was aflame. Spark arresters on portable sawmill burners and logging engines were only half effective. Woods were continually catching on fire, putting logging operators out of business and logging crews out of work. When a fire started, the logging crew might flee for their lives, after leaving donkey engines with steam up.

Archie Binns in his book, "Roaring Land," tells of the "dark day" he experienced as a boy.

"That first summer brought the Dark Day to western Washington. From the Cascade Mountains to the Pacific the land was in darkness. Many people thought it was the end of the world, and it was, for some of them. Down toward the Columbia River one forest fire roared through two hundred and fifty thousand acres of timber, and there were others all the way to the Canadian border. A lightship rolled at her mooring, with lights burning day and night and whistle bellowing unceasingly. Ships with coughing and tearful crews groped their way in toward the coast through a pall of smoke that extended forty miles to sea. Towns in the path of the fire storm disappeared forever and their names are forgotten. Families loaded what they could into their wagons and drove away, stunned and wandering aimlessly in the gloom of smoke and falling ashes. A mother and her children suffocated in a cave twenty yards from safety. And, as a final touch of terror, two desperadoes cruised in the pall of smoke, robbing and murdering and giving the slip to pursuers who were blindfolded by the dark.

"Eyewitnesses of the Dark Day are limited by the fact that in the hours of daylight people could not see far enough to recognize each other at a distance of a few feet. My own recollection is of seeing disembodied lamp flames burning in the gloom of the kitchen without illuminating anything, while Mother called attention to the fact that it was noon and the cows had come home and the chickens gone to roost. That afternoon a neighbor came through the woods from the salt water to see if we had escaped being burned to death. He was wearing an oilskin coat and sou'wester, and he carried a lighted lantern. The lantern in the middle of the afternoon showed what had been, and the oilskins foretold what would be. Rain had already begun to fall and by another day it had washed clean the blackened sky; but the rains of forty years have not cleared away the blackness from skeleton trees left by that fire."

"Fire in the timber" was catastrophe unless deliberately set for burning slash which was formerly mandatory. Slash fires however were usually kept under control. This is not a spectacular forest fire photo but a fine view of a "captive" fire burning hillside slash and held at timber's edge.

Stalwarts of the hemlock family on a Washington hilltop.

POLE ROAD. This method was a rather common type of hauling in some sections around 1910, an early effort to get logs "off the ground." Trucks used concave wheels and moderate loads were hauled by two or three horses. The two small photographs show first conversion of Fordson farm tractor to pole road logging in 1923 by Skagit Steel and Iron Works, as used by Scott Brothers Logging Co. at Van Horn, Washington, above Concrete. These Fordson "lokies" were made to run over rough tracks with little regard for curves. Timber used for rails was No. 1 stock.

"LITTLE TUGGER." MAC "lokey" made from Fordson tractor and forerunner of gasoline yarder. In 1921, Charles Brown of Bloedel-Donovan at Alger, Washington, wanted to log out some dead-and-down cedar for shingle bolts and needed light yarder which could be quickly moved around in timber. Skagit Steel and Iron Works built this experimental conversion—the first gas yarder—by taking back wheels off tractor and installing level drum set with direct connected gears. Some of these MAC yarders are still being used.

Salt water sawmill log boom. Boom men were expert at leaping from log to log and separating them for poling to mill.

Spike-team hauling five cars of shingle bolts on level grade.

There is a forest drama here. The three firs grew over the fallen cedar, were cut and burned in forest fire. All this time, for a total of 1380 years, the cedar log remained sound, although split and weathered. Section where man is standing was cut out to count rings of growth. Cedar log was 5½ feet in diameter—largest fir stump 10½ feet. The choicest of this old, naturally seasoned cedar was often used as violin stock.

CAT ROAD. These rangy crawler-type tractors could and can bring out logs ''standing on their heads.'' They made possible the ''gyppo'' or contract logger and selective method of logging. Best Tractor Co. was merged with the Holt, to form the present Caterpillar Tractor Co.

Early gas and tractor team at Hama Hama Logging Co. near Bremerton. This tractor and yarder combination gave loggers highly mobile, easily maneuvered yarding equipment and tolled the death knell of the steam donkey. Winches on tractors were later developed by Skagit and Pacific Car and Foundry Co. into invaluable additions to yarding equipment which went on to heavy diesel power. The "level drum" arrangement on yarder was modified to the "waterfall" with one drum higher so lines did not interfere with each other.

STEAM FALLER. Fallers continued to work by hand in spite of the efforts and hopes of the inventor of this steam falling saw, one of the many attempts to mechanize the falling operation. Drag saw was propelled by piston fed from steam line. As saw cut into tree it passed along curved segment but evidently required a man to hold it tight against sawed line. Note wedge driven in cut behind saw. In recent years some shingle manufacturers have salvaged cedar in old burned or abandoned high stumps, the wood being sound and usable.

Power Saw Pioneering

ATTEMPTS to replace manpower with machine driven saws in lumber falling and bucking were begun as early as 1879 with the Ransome steam tree faller. Most of the early efforts were related to the dragsaw or pitman type of machine, with gasoline, steam and air power. *The Timberman* of October, 1949, carried a creditable article on the evolution of the modern chain saw along the following lines.

In Henry Meddle's greenhouse near Sequoia Park in Eureka, California, in 1905, occurred the first experiment with a gasoline chain saw. The name of the inventor is not known. The saw was driven by a two-cylinder, water-cooled marine-type motor set at 90 degrees from its normal position. A tank cooling system was suspended on the tree above the motor.

In 1918, George W Wolfe, former logging boss of Red River Lumber Co. of Westwood, California, developed an early pitman type gasoline power saw. The works were mounted on a frame measuring 4½ x 6 feet. Power was furnished by a two-cylinder, two-cycle gasoline motor developing 6 horsepower The saw was designed to cut on the return stroke (22 inches) of the blade. The carriage was driven by two ¾-inch pitch screws. The chain drive was carried on two sprockets on a keyed shaft which directed the lateral movement of the carriage toward the cut. The saw blade had a gauge of 6 on the teeth and 12 on the back to prevent it pinching in the cut. The machine was said to have had a number of successful days during which 80,000 feet were felled in 10 hours. Saw weighed 210 pounds.

1919, in Portland, saw F. T. Dunham of Hoquiam, Washington, demonstrating a light weight air driven pitman type saw at the Pacific Logging Congress. George L. Kraber also exhibited his experimental air faller. The Arschau Dow Saw with gasoline engine mounted on a cart, was shown in operation at the P. L. C. in 1923. The Dow Pump and Engine Co. of California evolved a rugged powerful chain saw for performance in the pine country around 1935. Wheel mounted, limited in facility, it nevertheless had an excellent record of falling and bucking 70,000 feet daily for 36 days at the Lamm Lumber Co., Modoc Point, Oregon.

Saw makers Atkins and Disston entered the field, the former introducing an electric model powered by sled-mounted generator or tractor. Germany contributed the Stihl and Dolmar saws. Also building power saws was the firm of Spear and Jackson in Portland, and Reed-Prentice of Vancouver. The Slade Engineering Works manufactured a number of light falling saws and a few one-man bucking saws using the English Villiers six-horsepower motor.

Tractor yarding pair of logs at Campbell Logging Camp, Woodinville, Washington. Shown also is 10 x 12 compound geared yarder. Straight geared yarder used ¾″ to ⅞″ line and in order to eliminate blocking, the Puget Sound Iron and Steel Co. developed a 9¼ x 10 compound geared yarder. Engines of this type were produced by Willamette Iron and Steel Works, 11 x 13, and Washington Iron Works, 10½ x 10¼. Each of these used a 1¼″ line.

GOODBYE LINE HORSE. Yarding donkey and turn of logs on fore-and-after skid road bridge. The powered haulback line caused the line horse to lose his job of hauling the free line back for another turn of logs. Fore-and-after style of skidding shown on page 115.

Stevens, writer of the Paul Bunyan legends and lumber association consultant, in the Four L Lumber News of March, 1927. (It is interesting to note here that this publication was the official organ of the Loyal Legion of Loggers and Lumbermen and edited by Stewart H. Holbrook, noted for his *Holy Old Mackinaw* and other books of human enterprise. Harris Ellsworth, later a Roseburg, Oregon, newspaper man and representative in Congress, was advertising manager.) James Stevens wrote:

"The old Humboldt, which, before the Aberdeen fire, stood on the corner of Heron and South F streets, was a saloon conducted along hardboiled but strictly honest lines by 'Big Fred' Hewett. The Humboldt was a place for honest drinking and honest performing; a logger's life was perfectly safe inside its doors. In the Humboldt no gambler could bilk him out of his hard-made earnings. No painted dancer could spill chloral in his whiskey glass. No tin-eared plug-ugly could sock him behind the ear and

Poles and piling. These tall, slender firs reached extreme length
without appreciable tapering.

"OFF TO SEE AUNT MARY." Like some oversize bug or a stranded sled, this 1908 donkey pauses before pitching its skids over a log landing. It is maneuvering itself to a new location and the crews take time out for pictures.

then frisk his pockets. If the logger himself began to yearn for battle after a few drinks he soon found himself bouncing over the sidewalk outside, with Big Fred's voice roaring behind him, 'Come back when you want to be decent! I do all the fightin' for this place!'

"The old-time loggers knew the Humboldt as a trusty bank. When they flooded in from the woods before the Fourth of July and Christmas the big safe often held as much as $20,000, the deposits of loggers who wanted to protect themselves from the cutthroats and harpies. Each man's money was put in a separate envelope. His name and the sum was marked down until the whole sum was gone. When the logger got work-hungry, the Humboldt supplied him with a bottle to carry back to the woods and 'sober up on' before he took to the axe and saw again.

No depositor could draw from his envelope when he was drunk, not even for money to spend over the bar of the Humboldt. Big Fred Hewett's banking regulations were few, but they were strict; his banking system was simple but it worked. In one year he cashed $600,000 worth of checks.

"Like every other old-time western saloon of good fame, the Humboldt had an educational feature. Usually such features were along sporting lines. The walls would be full of pictures of famous pugilists of the past and of the present, photographs taken at the ringside of championship fights, gloves and trunks used by famous fighters, and so forth. Or a saloon-keeper might make a hobby of collecting racetrack trophies and photographs. Others were patrons of the arts and adorned their walls with gaudy oil

Fore-and-after skidding down a mountainside in 1914. The greatest problem in logging was, and is, how to get the logs out of the woods. At high elevations or in dense forests, railroads were often too difficult or too expensive to build. Before the day of light, mobile yarders, logs had to be pulled out on the ground. Contrary to uninformed belief, the trough of the fore-and-after formed by the three logs was not a chute in which logs slid down under their own weight. They were usually hauled by steam-powered lines, with a sled or hollowed-out log chained to the tail, nicknamed "pig," on which a man rode with a pike pole to keep the logs from snagging and to grease skids. These trough logs would be prime market supply today.

TRACKS TO THE CLOUDS. Incline railways were often the only way to get logs down steep mountain slopes without splintering or splitting timber. Loaded car is seen near the top of this 62% grade being lowered by donkey engine a thousand feet farther up. Engine pulled empty cars up grade and lowered loaded cars. Switch at bottom was always open to the siding to derail any runaway cars in case of cable breaking.

paintings, mostly of ladies more or less draped. But Fred Hewett had a hobby that finally made his saloon a sort of scientific educational institution for the loggers who frequented it. At last his collection became so important that eastern ethnologists heard of it, and high-toned visitors to Aberdeen who were interested in ethnology and natural history came to the Humboldt and risked getting their patent leathers punctured by calks while they looked over the Hewett collection.

"Sailors making the port on lumber-carrying schooners and steamers learned of Hewett's hobby and curious articles were brought to him from all over the world. So he even got pieces of mineral from every mining region on earth, two of them pieces of diamond ore containing bits of the valuable sparklers. Tribal garb, weapons and fishing gear came to him from the Philippine Islands and the islands of the South Seas. Tartars, Manchurians and Australian bushmen contributed to the cases along the walls of the Humboldt. Indians, from the Blackfeet to those of Mexico, had their weapons, bits of clothing and 'medicine' added to the collection. Whales and bugs, moose and snakes, parrots and owls joined the collection. The interlacing antlers of moose and elk heads made a border of horns along one wall. There was a galaxy of guns, of every imaginable style and period. Many of them had belonged to great hunters and fighters and had thrilling histories. So it was with the revolver collection and the knife collection. There was a gallery of curios; old coins, rare stamps, photographs of the early days of bull team logging, photographs of murderers and of the murdered, of an outlaw who died with his boots on —and those very same boots on exhibition, too; there were freaks of nature preserved in formaldehyde, a section of a stump which had been cut with a stone axe, and alder log which had grown around a scythe hung in the tree by some early settler. The Hewett collection in the end won recognition as making one of the best private museums in the country."

Throughout the forty years of Darius Kin-

Loggers at Lyman Timber Co., Hamilton, Washington, being hauled to work by incline cable. Heavy loads on these inclines were lowered down grade, one car at a time, empty cars hauled up. Therefore trestles could be lightly built.

Incline logging technique improved with the years through more skillful use of greater powered engines. Incline at Ebey Logging Co. Camp 3, Arlington, Washington, was a mile long and used block car shown above. Cable at left was anchored to a big stump, passed through sheaves and two pulleys on car to steam donkey at top of incline. Note block car is pulling locomotive and car of men up grade. Similar type of block car used at Dempsey Logging Camp at Hamilton, Washington [below]. This car was made by Pacific Car and Foundry Co., a pioneer in rail logging trucks and cars, building the first "long car" as distinguished from unconnected trucks.

Crews going to work on 48 per cent incline at Clear Lake Lumber Co. Block car is at top of grade. There were many incline operations in the Skagit River area. Hugh Sessions, who managed Marysville and Arlington Railroad for McEwan Bros. in 1908, invented a "lowering car" for steep grades. Danaher Lumber Co. at Darrington used similar incline.

sey's activities in the woods, Tib Kinsey was in charge of the thriving studio, turning out prints in "wholesale quantities" to be sent back to her husband and the loggers. When colored prints became popular, she applied herself to tinting and became highly skilled. There were many helpers in the studio — sixteen people working with the negatives and prints during one rush period — and the Kinsey home became known

familiarly as "Kinsey's Free Hotel." Pickup of supplies from Anderson Photo Supply and Lowman and Hanford, as well as trips to post office and express office, were continually being made. And there was always the classifying and filing of negatives.

In 1908 the demand for stereoptican slides and other prints had reached such proportions that a focal point in Seattle was necessary. A

Mountainside Railroad

RAILROAD INCLINE in Clear Lake Lumber Co. operation, in its day the largest inland logging and sawmilling company in Washington—long since dissolved The following description is from the company's booklet, "Travelog," of many years ago

"The speeder runs up the canyon of Day Creek, taking a maximum grade of 5 per cent, through rock cuts and over bridges, on the main line to the abandoned site of Camp 4 The car holds to the track, of course; for if not, it would plunge to the bottom of the Day Creek gorge a thousand feet below This cleft in the mountains is very much like that of the great White Pass, which reveals the river so far away that it is only the semblance of a silvery ribbon, unreal and beautiful in its apparent minuteness but stupendous and majestic because of its setting. From this location on the Clear Lake road one may view the Skagit River, and from the top of Haystack Mountain, a rocky cliff more than 4,100 feet high, there is a prospect unsurpassed anywhere, with Mount Baker in the center of the picture.

"From old Camp 4 the road doubles back, climbing higher and higher; then it switches back again, until it reaches the foot of the incline. At this place the speeder loses its usefulness, but it has accomplished its purpose in having landed the visitors at the vital point of the Clear Lake workings, for the incline is celebrated as the show-spot of the operation, where the presumption of man does a little better than measure up to the mightiness of Nature's obstacles he seeks to overcome.

"The Clear Lake incline is a railroad running straight up the mountain side. The length is 2,400 feet The perpendicular rise is not far from 1,600 feet. The first pitch is over a grade of 38 per cent, and the second pitch a grade of 40 per cent At the top of the incline is a Washington Iron Works snubbing machine 12 x 14, with drum and water-cooled brake bands like those on a mine-hoist, and from the drum is played a great steel cable along which is operated a lowering car with twin sheave wheels like the car built some years ago by the Willamette Iron Works for Sessons, who first applied the idea. Along the track are parallel wires, through which the operators signal to the snubbing machine simply by contact with an iron bar. Up this incline the other day went all the thirteen cars and equipment of Camp 4, and down it every work day go the loaded logging trains, two cars at a time. The incline has handled fifty cars in a day of eight hours. When a car is released at the foot it runs by gravity into a switch, and when again released there it runs by gravity in the opposite direction to the main track, where it is picked up by a logging locomotive for transfer to the make-up at Potts Station. The engineering features are not merely successful—they are spectacular "

Cold deck at Lyman Timber Co., Hamilton, Washington, of which C. J. Larson was contractor, in 1939. This operation utilized the North Bend system for pulling the logs from temporary stock pile or "cold deck." This consisted of a carriage on a skyline with the hauling line running through the fall block up and over a sheave in the carriage and back to the fall block and dead ended. When the turn was started in, the end of the log was raised so that it might pass over any obstruction.

home was purchased at 1607 East Alder Street and again became studio as well under the name Timber Views Company. Later in a larger home at 5811 Greenwood Avenue, the entire second floor was converted into photo processing quarters.

One day in the fall of 1940, Darius Kinsey set about to make a series of pictures in one of the logging camps. He had contacted the loggers' labor supplier Archie McDougal, checked on the work situation at the camp he intended to visit

and arrived safely. On the first day, he climbed a stump to operate the camera, slipped and fell, breaking several ribs. It was his last job in the woods. When he recovered, he took his family on several trips to Yosemite National Park, Niagara Falls and Washington, D. C., making many views for stereoptican use. The next five years were spent in marketing prints of the negatives he had accumulated and in other photographic activities. His last day, at the age of 74, came in 1945.

Men appear like bugs on this cold deck around spar tree. An estimated million and a quarter feet of lumber in this pile—two to three weeks' cut for the average mill of this period.

Two cold decks at Camp 1 Crescent Logging Co. on Olympic Peninsula. This operation was owned by Joe Irving, pioneer Everett logger, and used Port Angeles and Western Railroad. With Milt Stephens, he owned logging road out of Monroe up Skykomish River. [Below] Million feet of fir and cedar in this cold deck of Canyon Creek Logging Co., Granite Falls, Washington.

PATTERNS IN POLES. [Above] Crew of logging train paused for pictures on their 100-foot trestle. [Left] Temporary trestle of Clear Lake Lumber Co. over logged off area. Usual logging method was to cut close to camp first and extend roads and tracks into the timber farther away. Trestles were rarely torn down after logging off an area although steel was usually taken up. [Opposite] 593-foot railroad trestle over Cedar River canyon near Selleck, Washington. 203 feet high—built of fir poles to bring logs out of woods. Camera caught all details in network of 100-foot poles and braces. Trestle was built in two sections, upper one beginning at top of inverted V in center. Kinsey collection numbers dozens of these trestles, some using half a million feet of merchantable timber.

Marvels in Timber Engineering

THE wooden railroad bridges of the Pacific Northwest represented remarkable engineering feats. One of the most spectacular was the Baird Creek trestle of Weyerhaeuser Timber Co. on its Longview line. This all-timber structure was 1130 feet in length and rose 235 feet above the level of Baird Creek. Over 400,000 feet of treated timber went into the bridge, together with more than 200,000 feet of piling and other untreated members.

The Baird Creek bridge consisted of an untreated pile bent approach 250 feet long; next a center section composed of a three-hinge treated timber arch surmounted by a frame bent superstructure 480 feet long; and then another approach of driven pile bents 400 feet long, making a total length of 1130 feet. The width of the arch was 120 feet and its height 105 feet above the low water level of Baird Creek. On the steep slope of the east bank, apparently an old slide, four panels of driven treated piles were provided to carry the superstructure at this point. The piling on the shorter west approach was set into holes in the rock and grouted with concrete.

Surmounting the treated timber arch were four framed stories 30' each in height. Each bent consisted of five post members 14" x 16" corresponding in size to main members of the arch. Sway bracing was 3" x 10" and all girts were 6" x 12". Piles used in the span were 14" in diameter at the cutoff and ranged up to 120' in length on the west approach. Wood girders were 31" deep, placed three in a chord.

The Baird Creek span gave access to a big body of timber in the Kalama River Basin, destined to feed the mills at Longview for 20 years or more. Walter J. Ryan, long with Weyerhaeuser Timber Co., was chief engineer on this project.

RAISING A SPAR. The spar tree was the focal point of all high lead logging, as well as the slack line, North Bend and Tyler. All but high lead used tail spar also. A standing tree was chosen for its height, sometimes 150 feet or 200 feet high, and straight, well-rooted sturdiness. The purpose of height was to get the wire lines up in the air so logs being "swung" or yarded would not hang up on trees and other obstructions. When timber in the area was cut out, the spar trees were often left standing, bare of blocks. When a new "side" or logging site was being opened and a good tree was not growing where donkey must be placed, the spar was cut at ground level and moved to a new location.

Locomotives in the Timber

STEAM LOCOMOTIVES in the earlier days of the western logging industry were light, direct-connected engines as small as 10 to 15 tons. The geared engine was required to cope with the steep grades as the timberline was followed up the rugged mountain slopes. Geared engines were in use on the Pacific Coast for over 50 years. Three types vied for favor, these being the Shay, the Heisler and the Climax. These were distinguished by their distinct types of propulsion. The Heisler had its cylinders set at an angle directly under the boiler after the fashion of a V-type gasoline motor, driving a center shaft which in turn was geared to the trucks.

The Climax had two outside cylinders set at an angle of about 45 degrees, driving an articulated gear assembly. The Shay featured an off-center boiler placement, balanced by the three-cylinder engine and gear drive on the other side. Following the expiration of the Lima-Shay patents in the late '20s, Willamette Iron & Steel Works of Portland built several engines along the lines of the Shay, making it the fourth in the field of geared engines.

For speed on the mainline, direct connected engines were favored and in many cases, the geared locomotive served to pull the loaded cars off the steep spurs, delivering their loads to the rod engines when the mainline was reached.

Among the earliest types used in the woods was the Falk No. 1, operated by Elk Mill and Lumber Co. at Falk, California, in the '90s. A little later the Crown-Willamette Paper Company used a Climax geared locomotive No. 405 on its Youngs River operations. An early Shay was used on the line of the Benson Logging and Lumber Co. near Oak Point, Washington, below the present site of Longview.

In 1917 the logging railroad mileage had climbed to 3,853, over which operators were using nearly 8,000 sets of disconnected trucks and more than 5,500 flat cars. There were 593 geared locomotives in service that year and 267 direct connected engines making a total 859 pieces of motive power

Another census taken 10 years later in 1927, showed 6,164 miles of logging railroad and 740 miles under construction at the time of the survey The number of geared engines had risen to 825 and the roster of rod engines to 316. Rolling stock totals showed 10,500 sets of disconnected trucks and 5,500 flats.

Another sampling of the logging railroad situation was made in 1931 at which time the mileage was found to have reached a total of more than 7,200 miles. In service that year were 756 geared engines and 345 rod engines, for a total of 1,101. There were 340 individual logging roads in existence at this high point of railroading.

Heavy-duty Lima-Shay geared engines were used by the Clark and Wilson Lumber Company, hauling logs from Melalum Valley to log dump at Scappoose, Oregon. Later Willamette Iron and Steel Works built a 90-ton engine for the Eufaula Company, subsidiary of the former Eastern and Western Lumber Company A number of these locomotives continue in service although no longer built.

The Baldwin Locomotive Works produced many directed-converted engines like the 2-8-2 for fast mainline service. It also built a powerful compound engine, 2-6-0+0-6-2 with water supply in a saddle tank, using no tender. A saddle tank type was built for many West Coast timber operators by American Locomotive Works. The Porter was another locomotive used for the long haul.

Trailer Railroad

"I HAPPENED to be tending hook for the Forks Logging Co. in Monroe, Washington," said C. C. McLean in an article in *The Timberman*, August 1933. (See opposite top.) "F. R. Pendleton was manager. The show was very steep and in order to bring the logs to Snohomish River, Pendleton installed a trailing railroad about five miles in length, pretty fairly straight and averaging about 14 per cent grade. The line was built according to the usual standards of logging railroad construction, but instead of loading the logs on cars we made up the turns and trailed the logs behind a 45-ton Climax locomotive. The ties were spaced 10 to 18-inch centers.

"We would make up turns consisting of 12 to 14 logs, averaging about 1800 feet to the log, 32 to 40 feet in length. The logs were dogged together with grabs. The locomotive would couple to the head log and back down to the river at a speed of probably five miles per hour. Two 2 x 12 planks were spiked to insure the ties would not spread if a knot on the lower side might happen to strike the tie, otherwise there was no particular reason for planking the bridges. The turns would average from 15,000 to 32,000 feet, depending upon the size of the logs. The locomotive with her turn made six round trips per day. About 100,000,000 feet were taken over the road and the annual input was about 40,000,000 feet.

"The camp was afterward sold to the High Rock Logging Co. and later transferred to the Stevens-Bird Logging Co., Monroe, Washington, who finished the job, later installing a standard gauge railroad, using Milwaukee cars.

"There are times when logging on steep grades involves difficulties, especially when the weather is

Old No. 2 Shay locomotive of Knight and Company, trailing a turn of logs along ties between rails.

frosty. I well remember one morning the locomotive was headed from the landing to the woods. We had made up part of a turn the night before. This turn had a 7000-foot butt log at the head end which had not been coupled to the second log. The donkey engineer, pulling in his first log in the morning, bumped the partly made-up turn, which shoved the big log ahead on the frosty ties and headed it for the landing. I knew that unless the log was stopped it would collide with the locomotive, which was on its way back for another turn. I grabbed an empty powder box, filling it with loose earth and lying outstretched on the log, spilled the earth on the ties ahead of the bouncing log in order to check its gathering speed. At times I had difficulty in sticking to the log, which attained a momentum too great for me to jump, and forcing me to stick. The log traveled about one mile, where it reached a level spot in the track and slackened its pace. I jumped off and threw enough sand in front of the log to bring it to a full stop. The locomotive engineer and brakeman never knew how near they came to being swept off the track, but in this world we often worry about things that never happen, and a miss was as good as a mile in this case."

Loading Bottleneck

WHEN railroads first came into the woods, logs were loaded on disconnected rail trucks to be transported to mills. A rollway landing was built at foot of skid road, logs pulled up on it and then rolled out on set of tracks. This created a big logging bottleneck and the problem of getting logs on cars quicker and more economically.

To relieve this bottleneck, Washington Iron Works developed a duplex loader in 1915. This was a 7 x 10¼ engine, consisting of two sets of engines, with one loading drum mounted above the other and a car spotting drum mounted on the same shaft as the lower loading drum. This drum was controlled by a screw friction. Engines were reversing and one throttle handled each loading line, operating through a block or jack on the guy line directly over the car, with tongs or end hooks attached to a line from each loading drum. These lines were carried on a guy line and spread about 25 feet apart. In this way the log could be snaked out from a pile with one set of hooks and the other set of hooks placed on them and the log placed on the car. This increased the capacity of loading at least 20%.

Crews of Forks Logging Co., Monroe, Washington, could notch a line around the ends of big logs, set them on the rails and the 45-ton Climax would skid them out. Operation is described on page 127 by C. C. McLean, hook tender at this camp.

Thirty-four-car train of logs with pusher engine leaving Siler Logging Co. woods for tidewater dump. Head engine was heavier "road type" than ordinarily used in woods. Harry Siler built road from Silvana to Monroe up the Skykomish River with headquarters at Florence, known as the "Florence Road."

Loading operation at Florence Logging Co. landing in stand of fine fir near Monroe, Washington. Donkey set at extreme left. System here was "guy line," the simplest and most inexpensive. Most other loading systems used booms, such as McLean or "hayrack" and heel boom methods.

DRY LAND SAILORS. Log was hollowed out to haul men and tools up and down log chute or steep skid roads.

MOVING DAY. Cherry Valley Logging Co. moves camp to new show. Bunkhouses of larger logging firms were homes on wheels and some are still used as private dwellings today. Modern logging, with truck transportation and private automobiles for loggers, has eliminated most camps.

Rear view of double header logging train, one log to each car—1906 view. Small standing trees are refuse hemlocks in the logged off area.

[Opposite, below] Hand made chain-drive steam locomotive on narrow gauge track. However "homespun" these engine adaptations were, they gave small logging operators definite advantage of speed over horses. One advantage was they burned wood available on every hand instead of expensive hay. In 1890, at Monte Cristo on the South Fork of the Stillaguamish River, near the scene of this photograph, John D. Rockefeller built a sawmill and railroad called "Hartford Eastern." Rucker Bros. of Everett later took this over. This firm operated a mill at Lake Stevens and built Big 4 Inn, a resort hotel in the mountains. Speeders with small passenger coaches took guests up steep grades to hotel. [Opposite, above] Necessity in the woods bred handy men. This hand made locomotive could haul big loads on fairly level grade.

Early Logging in California

Darius Kinsey took few, if any, photographs in California logging camps, although he made trips to Yosemite and through the Redwoods. However, in his time there were many Washington loggers going into California operations.

There were the T. B. Walker enterprises in Westwood, reminiscent of the famous Susanville Ultimatum in 1912. The five Walker sons formed the Red River Logging Company. The Hammond interests were in Humboldt County at Samoa and furnished the background for the filming of Peter B. Kyne's story, "Valley of the Giants" with Wallace Reid. In 1880 Dolbeer (inventor of the steam donkey) and Carson had a mill at Eureka, logging redwood on the Eel River with horses. The old Dolbeer home was a landmark in Eureka for many years.

Diamond Match Company had its logging headquarters at Chico with logging near Sterling City and Butte Meadows in the foothills of the Sierras. Dick Colgan was manager, Dana Bailey logging boss.

In the early 1900s Charley Murphy was manager of Weed Lumber Company, logging Mt. Shasta National Forest. Long-Bell acquired properties at Fort Bragg, Mendocino County. Here Johnson Brothers formed Union Lumber Company. Wheelrites and Olds of Corry, Pennsylvania, had timber holdings in Jackson County, Oregon, and Siskiyou County, California.

In 1912, Sumner Bump, manager of Fruit Grower's Supply Company at Susanville, was putting into practice what he had learned from the French Government about forest conservation. At Scotia, the Pacific Lumber Company had the biggest mill in the redwoods and extensive railroad lines into the timber at Freshwater and Bull Creek Flats with incline at Monument Creek. In 1915 Swayne had a mill at Oroville and was logging in Merrimac County between the North and Middle Forks of Feather River with Pat Lyons as logging boss.

43,462 feet of lumber in four logs. Climax locomotive of Clear Lake Lumber Co. pulling four cars of logs away from landing; a single log to a car. Similar load at right — English Logging Co. Big logs were "sniped" or beveled at ends for easier skidding over rough ground and skid roads. In 1908 car trucks were still unconnected except by small logs to which load was chained. Clear Lake Lumber Co. mill was owned by B. R. Lewis who extended the logging road to Hamilton—originally built by George Miller up the river from Clear Lake.

CHERRY PICKER. Ronald MacDonald of the Cherry Valley Logging Co. designed and built a so-called "Cherry Picker." This device was a mobile crane and lifted the logs bodily with a hook on each end and placed them on cars. In the case of heavy logs, one end was lifted at a time as in photo of Bloedel-Donovan Beaver camp, next page.

[Above] Nine-foot fir log balanced on landing slip at an angle of 45 degrees. [Below] Mobile loader with steel boom at Bloedel-Donovan Beaver Camp.

[Opposite, above] Yarding on hillside. Wreckage above and to left of donkey was caused by logs up to twelve feet in diameter being yarded down slope in all directions. Note spark screen on stack. [Below] Loggers take recess as well as children — yarding small logs by Cletrac tractor with trailer around Washington school yard.

Fleet of early Diamond-T logging trucks at Utsalady on Camano Island, Washington, in 1920. [Below] Loading boom rigged to spar tree—truck logging method used in 1920. Rear set of Diamond-T truck wheels are part of trailer.

Trucks were just feeling their way into the woods when Kinsey took this picture in 1920. Loads were small because equipment, like this 6-wheel Diamond-T truck with long bed and solid tires [above] could not operate on steep grades or rough roads. Most of them were planked and the gulleys bridged with logs on which planks were laid lengthwise, forming at best precarious tracks against sure disaster. Most often restraining lines running from snubbing drums were used to brake them down steep grades. [Below] Loading Nash-Quad logging truck. Log on ground makes fuel for donkey. Hardly a wisp of smoke was lost in Kinsey's finer pieces of work.

Early Federal truck being eased down steep grade by wire rope. Solid tires required solid footing of logs and loads were light and short for limited length of truck bodies. [Below] Four Garford log trucks on temporary trestle, fourth truck an early dump-type. Trucks were chain driven, had solid beds, solid tires and usually required planked roads. Trestles like these were lightly built, of low cost and in direct contrast to the long, high trestles used by logging railroads. [Opposite] A high elevation hillside of hemlock logs for pulp and heavy-duty logging truck ready to start down grade. Lean-to near truck houses snubbing engine necessary to brake trucks on steep slopes. Once a waste wood, hemlock is now the mainstay of Washington logging industry, logged in gasoline and diesel operation, at high elevations and logs hauled out by trucks.

Log truck grows up. Improved, heavy-duty, trailer-type Diamond-T [above] carried bigger loads down steeper grades. Today's logging truck such as the Kenworth [below] has the capacity of a freight car and far greater utility. As truck logging progresses, timber firms build better roads and many of them today contract with hauling firms to truck logs to landings and mills.

[Opposite page] 15 Western red cedar trees averaging 8 feet in diameter, 75 to 100 feet high.

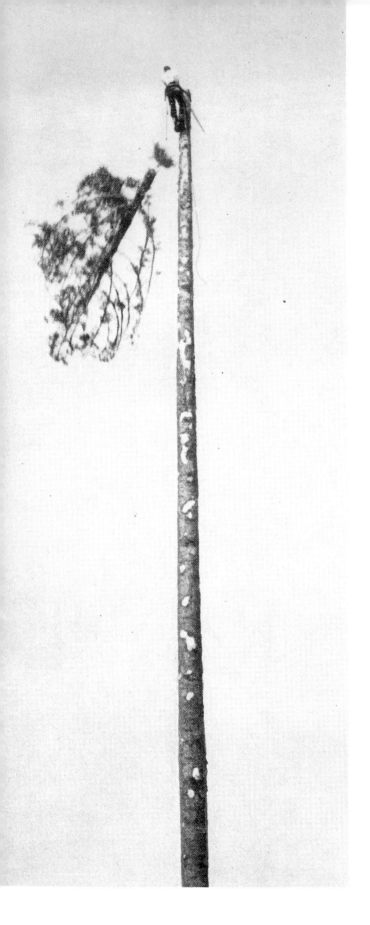

High Climber

THE high climber's job was the most spectacular and daring work in the woods, but not necessarily the most dangerous. It was his job to climb the tree picked for a spar, lop off limbs on his way up, with a one-man saw and topper's axe, and twenty-five or thirty feet from the top, loop himself to the tree with a rope. Then he cut the top off, hanging on precariously while the top fell over him, the tree whipping and twisting in a twenty-foot arc.

Well-known high climber was Philip Grabinski, who at one time held the Northwest spar tree climbing record, scaling a spar tree 150 feet high in one minute and three seconds, lowering himself to the ground in eighteen seconds. In *The Timberman* twenty years ago, while working in Weyerhaeuser Camp 1, Rainier, Washington, he described some of his experiences.

"The first tree I topped was at North Bend, Washington, and I was scared just enough to be very careful. I started up this tree, which was about five feet through, so it took about 22 feet of rope to go around the tree and my body. The tree was 180 feet high and 18 inches through on top, so it took about nine feet of rope up there. When I got ready to top I took a good look all around. I wanted to know where I'd be after the top started over and as soon as I saw all the spare rope that I had taken in as I went up the tree, I took it and threw it around the tree again. Having two ropes around me I felt much better immediately.

"When the top went it didn't even give me a thrill as it fell away from me. I thought this business was pretty easy till I topped the next one. It was a much larger tree and as I was chopping, my body was swinging on the long, sharp spurs. They kept working steadily deeper into the tree and pretty soon the top cracked and instead of going away from me as I had figured, it came right at me. When I tried to get around the tree I found my spurs so deep I couldn't get them out and right then and there I started thinking of many things, mostly about what a bad boy I had been.

"It was a heavy top and as it came over it pulled the whole trunk of the tree with it for 10 or 12 feet till the top was about 45 degrees, then it broke loose and the tree swung back with me. The top fell straight down and cleared me plenty, so now I know it is impossible to get hit with the top of a tree up there.

"There are quite a few cases of high riggers cutting their ropes while topping. Most all high riggers cut their ropes a little, possibly one or two strands, some time or other. A regular climber's rope consists of four strands of hemp over a soft wire core. Many people believe that the wire core in the rope makes it safe but an ordinary blow with a tree-topping axe will cut it in two as the wire has to be very soft to be usable in a rope.

"One reason why tree toppers do not cut their ropes more than they do is because when we are topping a tree we are chopping about three inches above the rope and striking lengthwise instead of crosswise. When we strike the rope it generally rolls with the axe bit, and only one or two strands are cut. When that happens we fix it before we go any further.

"One of several things may cause a rope to be cut. One spur may pull out of the tree when you are in the middle of an axe stroke or it may happen when topping on a windy day. We always try to fall our trees with the wind. That makes us stand so the wind strikes us sidewise and swings us around the tree. The tree is so small where it is being topped that our feet are right close together and we can't always brace ourselves as well as we should.

"The real hazard of topping trees comes in windy weather when there is danger of the tree splitting. If you get an undercut chopped into the tree and a gust of wind comes along and blows the top the other way, it is liable to split the tree down the heart. If the tree topper isn't fast about that time, and scampers down about 25 or 30 feet to where the split part breaks off, he is apt to be crushed against the tree by the rope and his back broken.

"I have had one tree split on me. Another close call was when a top fell into another tree nearby and kicked back and almost caught me. This incident was at Camp No. 1 of the St. Paul & Tacoma Lumber Co. at Kapowsin, Washington, and was witnessed by William McAbee, foreman of that camp.

"The fastest job of raising a tree I have ever witnessed or heard of was at St. Paul & Tacoma's Camp No. 1. I was climbing. Cecil Coleman was the hooker and Bill McAbee was the foreman.

"We put up a 172-foot spar tree in eight minutes from the time it left the ground till we ran the main line in and tree was tied with four guy wires and perfectly straight.

"The advantage of sawing over chopping in tree topping is that in sawing you cut just what is necessary to go through a tree about an eighth of an inch wide. In chopping you have to cut so much dead wood. In a 12-inch cut your opening starts out about 12 or 14 inches wide compared to a saw's one-eighth inch. With a saw you are cutting steadily while with an axe, only when the axe bit is in the wood are you doing any work.

"The reason most toppers use an axe is because they have to have the axe anyway for the undercut and the limbs. Then, too, the saw is dangerous to have hanging from your body when you chop a limb off, as it is liable to hit the saw as it falls and either jerk you up pretty hard or cause it to fly back and cut you, and it is too much to carry through the woods, with belt, rope, spurs and axe."

SETTING UP A SIDE. Hanging lines and buckle guys to new spar tree by three high riggers with snow on ground. Topping saw hangs on line at right of tree. This spar was a growing tree at Camp Pysht, Washington, on Olympic Peninsula. Tracks were laid, donkey moved in and after guy lines were set, tree shoe and blocks rigged. Merrill and Ring started logging in 1916, rafting logs through Straits of Juan de Fuca and Puget Sound to mills in Seattle.

WOOD BUCK. Firing early steam engine. Photograph gives an idea of the amount of good timber that was cut up for fuel. Later donkeys were fired by oil which saved much timber and eliminated the extra man called the "wood buck." Steam logging machinery has since been superseded by gasoline and diesel power and crews further reduced. [Opposite] High riggers setting lines to spar.

High lead operation at Ebey Logging Camp 3, Arlington, Washington, showing landing and method of loading logs on cars. Darius Kinsey notes that John Normark was foreman of this camp but does not identify him in the photograph.

HIGH LEAD. "Get the logs off the ground." The high lead system was the key to faster yarding, less power on the pull and elimination of end sniping of logs. High lead blocks as shown here were 100 to 150 feet above ground.

"Get the Logs Up!"

THE high lead logging method was born of the wasteful, expensive ground lead system. It eliminated the "hang ups" of logs pulled flat on the ground and was especially adapted to logging uphill which gave a lift to the logs, particularly in clear cut areas.

High lead still used the donkey engine but lines were now rigged to spar tree extending a quarter to half a mile into the timber. Spar trees were chosen for their tall straight sturdiness, topped and trimmed of

limbs, guy lines set to steady them under the terrific force of ten tons of flying logs. High lead blocks and lines were geared from spar tree out to a tail spar and along this high line ran the roller block from which dangled the choker shackles and logs. Loading blocks also operated on the spar for cold decking, or stock piling, and hoisting logs on railroad cars and later, trucks.

The slack line method was generally considered the best of the skyline systems. The log could be instantly elevated or lowered to allow for ground conditions and eliminated much log damage. "Roads" could be changed more quickly than with tight skyline systems such as North Bend and Tyler.

High lead and guy lines make maze of cables at this Sauk River Logging Co. operation. Full rigging consisted of six top guy wires, five buckle guy wires and all blocks. The Washington Iron Works steam skidder is 12 x 17 and duplex loader 10 x 12, with rigging engine on the front. The entire skidder was mounted on a Pacific Car and Foundry Co. steel car for easy transportation from one setting to another.

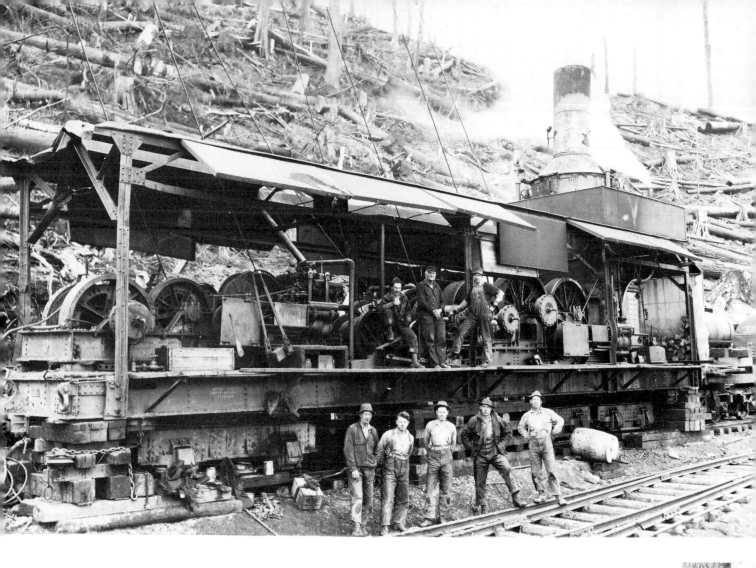

Car mounted Flyer used at English Camp 11 with two sets of engines—one main engine, one set for handling high lead line and one for main and haulback drums. Duplex loader is in center and rigging engine in front. In the early days, Ed English maintained a general store in Mt. Vernon and with the Butler interests of Everett helped many loggers buy timber. He owned much timber north of the Skagit River and to log it, joined with Lawrence Dempsey to build the "English Road" or Puget Sound and Baker River Railroad to Hamilton. [Right] Front view of Clyde steam skidder.

AERIAL TRAM. Detail of snubbing carriage built by Washington Iron Works for the Nestos Timber Co. in Bellingham. This carried logs from the top of the hill down across the river to the flat below. There was a knob secured to the line near the end which locked the carriage when the log was raised. By pulling on the line attached to the latch, the carriage was released and snubbed down the line with a load of logs by the engine. The trigger at the lower end of the line allowed logs to be lowered and the choker taken off. The hauling line was then pulled up to the carriage and the knob released the carriage to be returned to the top of the hill for another load. Then the carriage was pulled back to the tail tree again where it was held in place by the latch. Several of these were made since it worked very successfully.

[Left] As logs grew scarce in lowlands, hillside logging became necessary. Railway inclines were not always possible or too expensive. Logs were sometimes swung by means of a skyline with snubbing carriage. This carriage rode the cable quarter of mile down the steep slope and across the Nooksack River to railroad spur.

[Right] Duplex yarder and loader on North Fork of Skykomish River in Washington. Spar tree is 210 feet high and rigged for North Bend yarding system. Here, as in all tight line skyline systems, the skyline is anchored to a stump at the tail tree and a stump or heel block drum at the head tree. The load is divided between the main line and the skyline. Ordinarily, the logs drag along the ground, but when an obstacle is encountered, the fall block can be raised by holding the haulback line tight, thereby lifting the turn upward until the obstacle is cleared.

GOODBYE SPAR TREE. Big time log production hit its peak with the use of the tower skidder. The mountain of machinery moved into location on rail under its own power, carrying its own spar, with complex blocks and drums for yarding and loading. Steel spar skidders came to the Pacific Northwest about 1915 and at one time there were more than 100 units in use in the West plus many tree-rigged machines working essentially along the same lines. Lidgerwood Manufacturing Co. conceived the idea of a permanent steel spar and built the first ones 60 feet high, later 80 and finally 100 feet. For a time Lidgerwood skidders were built by Puget Sound Iron and Steel Co. in Tacoma. Willamette Iron and Steel Works built a 100-foot tower skidder for Crown-Zellerbach Corp. for use at Cathlamet, Washington. Washington Iron Works built one with electrically operated drums for Long-Bell Lumber Co. at Ryderwood, Washington. [Above] Steel tower skidder yarding and loading at Siler Logging Co. [Opposite] Similar equipment at unidentified locations.

MODERN DIESEL YARDER. As loggers had bigger gasoline and diesel equipment available to them, the larger donkeys were supplied with air controls as this Skagit yarder. Air compressor shown attached to diesel engine. And with good truck roads in, big fuel tanks could be mounted on skids.

Swinging gas yarder by slack line into an unopened logging area in 1925. Mounted on sled, yarder is slung from skyline carriage by choker shackles. In-haul line at left of carriage —out-haul at right.

Here are forty years of forestry in Douglas fir region, from 2000 feet up Blue Mountain, eastern Snohomish County, Washington. Darker areas are older second-growth fir and hemlock. Large, lighter areas are later cuttings, with new crops that have not closed in. Dark tree lands, mid-ground [left] are on land cut over in 1918. Some trees in view are third crop. With Cub Scouts who are putting up fire prevention posters, are forestry men Harry Osborn [left], William Entwhistle, Henry Knudsen and Jim Stevens. Photo courtesy West Coast Lumbermen's Association.

Early Oregon Logging

In 1914 two Minnesota lumber companies moved to Bend impounding the Deschutes River water for ponds—Brooks-Scanlon Lumber Company with Sam Blakely as manager and Shevlin-Hixon Company with Jack Meister as manager.

Both the Union Pacific Railroad and Great Northern fought for the right of way, both building track from the Columbia River. Workers laid rails with rifles handy. Excitement ran high at Madras, one contractor putting down steel while another tore it up. The war turned out to be bloodless as a truce was eventually signed and one track laid for both lines.

At Bend, Phil Brooks financed the building of the famous Pilot Butte Inn, with plate glass windows 20 feet long and 10 feet high, framing a beautiful mountain scene. 100 miles south on Klamath Lake, at Modoc Point, Lamm Lumber Company operated for over 50 years. A few miles north, at Chiloquim, on the Sprague River, E. A. Blocklinger, who pioneered logging for the Pacific Lumber Company, built a mill in 1920.

To Coos Bay in the early 1900s came Al Powers, an old Michigan river man, to organize the Smith-Powers Lumber Company at Marshfield with a logging road to Coquille and up the river to Myrtle Point. The company built splash dams and drove logs to Myrtle Point, railroaded them to Marshfield and shipped them by schooner to San Francisco. One ship was named *Nan Smith* for Powers' daughter. When he retired, the company became the Coos Bay Lumber Company.